Gordon Corrigan

Introduction

The Hundred Years War, that series of campaigns and battles that began with King Edward III's statement of claim to the throne of France as of right in 1337 until the withdrawal of English troops from France (except for Calais) in 1453, was not, of course, 116 years of constant fighting, rather it was a series of campaigns and battles punctuated by truces, some of them many years long. No one who stood on the docks of the River Orwell in Ipswich and cheered as the soldiers of the first English expeditionary force of the war sailed for France under Edward III in 1340 was alive to welcome the men returning from the last campaign of Castillon in 1453, and anyone living at the end of the war who could remember the great 1415 battle of Agincourt would be well into middle age. The period might more accurately be described as the series of events which transformed the English from being Anglo-Norman into pure Anglo, and citizens of duchies in France into Frenchmen, but in that the causes of the war and the English war aims remained more or less constant, even if alliances did not, it is reasonable to consider the series of struggles as one war. Although the three great battles of the war, Crécy, Poitiers and Agincourt are the ones that most of us remember, it was the less well known battle of Sluys in 1340 , a hybrid battle fought on ships in harbour, that ensured that a French invasion of England could not happen, and that the battles of the war would devastate the French countryside, burn French villages and level French fortresses, and not those of England.

The first land battle of consequence, Crécy, in August 1346, was a stunning English victory and it was another ten years before the Battle of Poitiers, the subject of this book, and an interval of another fifty-nine years before Agincourt. In the intervals between major battles where the main English army met the main French one, there were skirmishes, raids, sieges, political upheaval and religious strife. The war encompassed the reigns of five English kings and six French ones. English suspicions of the papacy did not begin with Henry VIII in the 1540s but was present long before that, when the English were convinced that the popes were puppets of the French, as from 1309 when the French pope Clement V moved the papal court to Avignon, they most certainly were. The next seven popes were all French, until the last of them, Gregory XI, moved back to Rome in 1376. Although his successor, Urban VI, was Italian he and those who came after him tended to support the French, on the very practical grounds that the French could invaded Italy but not England. In any case the English tended not to pay their Peter's Pence, an annual tithe paid to the church in Rome, on time or frequently not at all, and to whom the church was the first port of call when taxation to pay for the war was required.

The interval between Crécy and Poitiers was eventful indeed. It saw the coming to independent manhood of Edward the Black Prince, a teenage wing commander at Crécy and fully fledged army commander at Poitiers, it saw the capture and retention of Calais, and the dreadful ravages of the 'Black Death', bubonic plague that wiped out perhaps as much as fifty percent of the population of Europe, to say nothing of its effect in Asia and Africa. The sources for this period are plentiful, and whether written in ecclesiastic Latin, Norman French or Middle English they have survived and are easily available to the scholar in the National archives at Kew, the British Library at St Pancras and the French archives at Valenciennes and Paris. Norman French was still the preferred language of English royalty, although Edward III and his successors could speak English, still the language of the common folk, and it was not until Henry V that an English king spoke and wrote in English by preference, as well as to emphasise English national identity.

The Battle of Crécy was a great victory, but it did not end the war. This book continues the tale of the next ten years, dramatic as those years were.

Chapter One – After Crécy

The Battle of Crécy on 26 August 1346 was a great English victory. Nevertheless, although English casualties were minimal, having gone on well into the gathering dark the hours of fighting had exhausted the army. The wounded had to be attended to, the stocks of arrows replenished, either from the baggage train or by retrieving those already shot and the battlefield had to be gleaned to collect anything that might be reused or recycled. Loose horses had to be caught and those wounded put down[*], and the men had to be fed. As Edward had ordered his men not to take prisoners there were none to be guarded, but the army was in no state to pursue the remnants of the French forces. The king declared a truce to allow the heralds to identify the dead, and the local civilians to bury the common soldiers in mass graves, while the bodies of the royal household and senior nobles were taken to a nearby monastery. After three days the army was ready to march on, but there could be no question of staying in enemy territory any longer than necessary. The troops headed for home.

Public relations were as important in the fourteenth century as they are today. While England was far from being a democracy, the population had to be kept on side and supportive of the war. A suitably embellished account of the victory of Crécy was sent back to England. By the time the army was ready to move on, on either 29 or 30 August, it was being read out in every pulpit in the land. The people rejoiced and even the guardians of the national wealth in Parliament became less reluctant to find the money for continuation of hostilities. Not everyone at home was so enthusiastic. A glorious victory, at a small cost in casualties, was to be applauded, but where, wondered some parliamentarians, was the practical advantage? No prisoners were taken so there was no ransom money to be fed into the economy. The French showed no signs of surrendering the throne or of returning ancestral English

---

[*] Even today a horse with a broken leg cannot be made sound – it can only be put down.

lands. So, looked at in the cold light of day, devoid of patriotic emotion, where was the profit? Edward was well aware that if he was to retain the support of parliament and the great men of the kingdom, he had to show some practical gains. The answer might be to capture a city not previously in English hands and one which could be held, thus acquiring some permanence from the campaign.

Meanwhile in France the hunt for the guilty was well under way. While no one openly blamed the king, evil counsellors and corrupt officials must have played a part. The displeasure of the almighty, the weather, the unsportsmanlike behaviour of the English in using low born archers, all came in for some of the blame. Of course, it was always easy to blame the jews, particularly if they were denounced by someone who owed them money. The crossbowmen failed due to cowardice and were to be executed. Some were indeed despatched until it was pointed out that as they might be needed again, to kill them was counter-productive. French troops relatively quickly reoccupied the areas that the *chevauchée* passed through, and stern punishment was meted out to those Normans who had thrown in their lot with Edward, including the garrison of Caen, who were rounded up and executed. What no-one was prepared to admit, or at least not openly, was that in the face of disciplined dismounted infantry supported by a missile weapon French tactics were hopelessly out of date, and that refusal to recognise reality was to cost them dear in the years to come.

If King Edward was to return to England with a practical profit the obvious prize would be Calais. With a population of about 8,000 it was not then a town of any great commercial significance. Its harbour was small and liable to silt up and most travel between England and Europe was through Wissant or Boulogne, both of which had much better and more easily navigable approaches. But it was just across the channel from England, and had long been a nest of pirates who preyed on the ships of the wine trade from Bordeaux. It was rumoured to be very rich as a result. It was just north east of Edward's intended port of embarkation, and it was conveniently near Hainaut, friendly towards the English whose queen, Philippa, was the daughter of its count. However, it was strongly garrisoned by the French as a guard against incursions from Flanders, with sufficient stocks of food to withstand a long siege.

Heading north, the English army continued to do as much damage as it could while bypassing any town or village held in strength. By now almost everyone had a horse, either those brought over in the original landing or captured on the way to or on the battlefield of Crécy. On 2 September the army reached Sangatte, from where they could see Calais, having taken eight days to cover the 58 miles from Crécy. This may seem excessively slow for an all mounted army (today infantry on their feet could cover that distance in little more than a day) but with only farm tracks and the remnants of Roman roads to move along, and the requirement to forage for feed for the horses and to reduce any French villages along the way, it was not bad going for the time.

It is unlikely that Edward ever thought that he could take Calais by a *coup de main*, for it was well sited for defence. To the north was the harbour and the open sea, to the west was a river with only one bridge which could easily be demolished by the defenders, and to the east and south was marshland criss-crossed by streams and rivulets that constantly changed their courses. Within those natural defences were a series of well-constructed walls, themselves protected by moats, and at the western end was the castle, with its own separate system of walls, towers and ditches. Before the development of effective cannon, there were three ways of assaulting a walled city or castle: over the walls, through the walls or under the walls. Over the walls meant escalade – placing ladders against the wall for the attackers to climb up. Provided the defenders were not all asleep, this was a very hairy business indeed. The one-man ladders were light enough to be carried but easily pushed away and stones and boiling water could be dropped on the climbers. Even if one man managed to reach the top of the wall he was at a distinct disadvantage to the more numerous defenders. Another, more complicated method was by the use of a belfry, a three- or four-storey wooden tower on wheels or runners. Packed with archers and men-at-arms, it would be pushed towards the wall until the attackers could leap from the top storey of the belfry onto the wall. It was a very old stratagem – the Romans had made frequent use of belfries – and it took much time and labour to place it in position. Once packed with men, a belfry was very heavy and the ground had to be levelled and a road built to allow it to be pushed along. All this preparation would be obvious to the defenders, who would try to set the belfry on fire with fire arrows or throw burning balls of straw soaked in pitch at it, and mass their own men on the walls as it approached. While the belfry was still theoretically on the equipment tables of a medieval siege train, it was hardly ever actually built or used[*]. Through the walls meant bringing up a battering ram, usually a log with a metal tip on a carriage which allowed the ram to be swung back and forth against the wall, or occasionally the gate, although the latter was even better defended than the walls. Here the defenders would drop stones, shoot arrows and pour oil onto the ram and its crew, with flaming arrows used to ignite the oil. Again, a very chancy business and unlikely to succeed even if it did manage to collapse at least part of the wall. Under the walls meant tunnelling. Miners would start a tunnel out of sight of the defenders and dig it until they reached below the wall. The tunnel would be shored up by pit props and once under the wall a chamber would be excavated, the roof propped up and the whole filled with flammable material – dead pigs were favourite as they contained lots of fat. The fire would be lit, the miners would withdraw and the fire would destroy the pit props, causing the wall to collapse. That at least was the theory. In practice it took a very long time, it was difficult to calculate where the tunnel had got to, there were problems of ventilation and drainage and if detected by the defenders it could be collapsed by counter tunnelling. In any case tunnelling through rock was impossible and in marshy ground difficult and

---

[*] The French did make one for the siege of Breteuil in 1356. It took a month to fill in the moat and when the belfry was finally pushed up to the walls, the defenders set it on fire.

dangerous. That said the English, along with the Germans, were generally reckoned to be rather good at tunnelling, if it really had to be done*. The result of all this was that medieval fortifications were hardly ever taken by assault – rather starvation, disease or treachery delivered them up†. It was common for the commander of a fortified town or castle to agree that if a relieving force had not arrived by a certain date then he would surrender, generally considered to be perfectly honourable.

At Calais, going over or through the walls was not an option as the moats and ditches protected the approaches. Mining was out because of the waterlogged nature of the soil and siege engines were too heavy to be moved over the marshy ground. Starvation was the only answer and the English were quite prepared to settle down for a long siege. Reinforcements arrived from England and the fleet under Sir John de Montgomery, Admiral of the South, hove off to Calais at around the same time the army got there on land. The soldiers began to block off all roads and tracks running to and from the town and a vast camp was set up on the dry ground around the church of St Peter where the roads from Boulogne and Ardres crossed. The camp would have to be in position for the long term, so shops, armourers' tents, quarters for the nobility, butts for the archers, paddocks for the horses and all the facilities of a large town had to be constructed. While the army was on the move, it could feed itself from the French countryside, but now that it was static, the available food in the immediate area would soon be exhausted and provisions would have to be brought in from England.

---

* Thanks to their skill in tunnelling under walls, by royal decree of Edward I any male born within the Forest of Dean who had worked in a mine for a year and a day was granted the right to mine anywhere in the forest without a licence, a right still enjoyed today, although as most mines in the Forest of Dean are long closed, and boys are now born in the local hospital, which is not in the forest, there are fewer and fewer who are eligible.

† Edward's capture of Caen was an exception, but there the walls had already been allowed to collapse.

To supply the siege government agents went out all over southern England to purchase foodstuffs and other supplies for the army. These had to be found, collected, paid for, moved to the ports, loaded on ships – which themselves had to be impressed – and delivered to the army. The French scored a minor success when a fleet of galleys from the Seine intercepted one of the first supply convoys and sank or burned most of the ships, killing the crews and dumping the cargoes. Future convoys would have men-at-arms or archers on board and the supply line was never broken again, but the need to put soldiers on the ships did increase the expense of the logistic effort.

While arrangements for the siege of Calais were being put in place, and the king's agents were scouring the southern and eastern counties for supplies, the Scots decided to take a hand. Allied since the time of Edward I – 'The Auld Alliance' – the French now appealed to the Scots to do something to distract the English from following up their Crécy victory. The twenty-two year old Scottish King David II, son of Robert Bruce, who had been married to Edward III's sister Joanna at the age of four and had returned from exile in France in 1341, saw this as a good moment to attack their traditional enemy. Assuming that all the English soldiers were safely out of the way in France, David invaded England in early October 1346, a move generally popular with the Scottish magnates who assumed that the north of England was ripe for the plucking. Storming down the Roman road and pillaging as they went they took the castle of Liddel Strength, twelve miles north of Carlisle, and beheaded its captain, Sir Walter de Selby. At this point David's chief military adviser Sir William Douglas, the thirty-six year old Lord of Liddlesdale, advised that enough was enough, they had done what they promised the French that they would do, and it was now time to return over the border before retribution arrived. David rejected this sound advice, claiming that as all the English soldiers were in France, there was no one to oppose them but 'wretched monks, lewd priests, swineherds, cobblers and skinners'. The raid continued, and included the despoiling of the priory of Lanercost, twelve miles beyond Liddel Strength, which presumably accounts for the

Lanercost Chronicler's obvious hatred of the Scots, claiming as he does that King David and his men made a habit of defecating in the fonts of churches they passed, which given that the Scots were almost as terrified of the wrath of God (as opposed to that of his earthly representatives) as everyone else seems unlikely[*]. In assuming that England had nothing with which to reply to a Scottish incursion David was very wrong: Edward had not arrayed any troops north of the River Trent, and the defence of the Scottish marches had been entrusted to the very capable hands of William de la Zouche, the fifty-two year old Archbishop of York, Warden of the Marches and principal Commissioner of Array in the north, who mustered an army at Barnard Castle on 15 October before moving north to Bishop Auckland, south of Durham, the following day. The army numbered around 1,000 men-at-arms, 2,000 archers and 5,000 spearmen, against probably the same number or less of Scots. The usual three divisions were commanded by the Archbishop himself, Ralph, Lord Neville and Henry, Lord Percy. The Scots army was encamped in the priory grounds of Beaurepaire (still there, but now Bear Park), a few miles north of Durham when on the morning of 17 October 1346 a foraging party of around 400 Scots under Douglas ran into the Archbishop's vanguard in a thick mist and got very much the worst of the encounter, with only Douglas and half his men getting back to raise the alarm. The Battle of Neville's Cross which followed went on for most of the day . The Scots came on in the same old way, and the English archers on the wings slaughtered them in the same old way. When the lines of infantry met it was rapidly evident that the Scots could not hold and those officers and men on the Scots flanks began to flee the field leaving the king and his immediate household to fight on. The writer of the Lanercost

---

[*] In Professor Maxwell's translation of Lanercost, published in 1913, he refuses to translate that accusation, presumably on the grounds that it was not suitable for the more tender ears of the time. He does make the point that the chronicler continually shows 'monkish spite' against all things Scots – but then if your priory is plundered and burned every time the Scots cross the border, you would feel quite spiteful.

chronicle probably exaggerates the speed of desertion, but he says that Earl Patrick should have been named Earl 'Non Hic'[*], and in any event the Scots king and Sir William Douglas were taken prisoner and carted off to the Tower while the remnants of their army fled back to Scotland, not even stopping to defecate in fonts on the way. The captor of David received an annuity of £500 a year[†] and promotion to banneret. Brave but foolhardy, King David was said to have sustained two head wounds from arrows. The surgeons removed one but the arrowhead of the second remained lodged in his head for many years, until it popped out one day while he was at prayer – or so it was claimed.

Back at Calais a brief attempt to bring down the walls by hurling rocks at them with trebuchets, machines that relied on a counterweight on a beam with a huge sling on its end and which could deliver seriously large stones against or over a wall. This failed when the ground was too soft to allow a firm foundation for the trebuchets. An ingenious plan to assail the walls from boats fitted with scaling ladders was finally abandoned despite considerable expenditure in preparing the boats, and the blockade went on. Although the town was well provisioned its stores would not last forever and the commander of the garrison, Jean de Vienne, an experienced and competent officer, decide to eke out supplies by evicting his useless mouths, and so around 2,000 civilians – women, children, the old, the sick and the weak – were expelled into no-man's-land between the walls and the investing army. At first Edward would not allow them to pass through his lines, and as there was nothing for them to eat save what little they had managed to carry away with them, they soon began to die. Edward relented and the dispossessed were allowed passage through the siege lines. While no food could reach the garrison overland, and attempts to run supplies in by sea were usually

---

[*] Probably Sir Patrick Dunbar, and for the few readers whose Latin may be rusty, non hic means 'not here'.

[†] It is difficult to give a modern value to £500 in 1346, but then you could buy a fairly decent horse for £1.

prevented by the English navy, the occasional blockade runner did manage to reach the harbour, but the quantities that could be delivered by this means were small.

During the latter part of summer and autumn life within the English camp was reasonably comfortable, but with the onset of winter conditions began to deteriorate. An army on the move could keep reasonably healthy, but once it became static disease inevitably followed and Edward's army of 1346 was no exception. Little attention was paid to the cleanliness of water sources, latrine arrangements were primitive, flies and rats abounded and soon dysentery, 'the bloody flux', began to take its toll. Dysentery is an infection of the gut and is passed on by contact with an infected person or by touching or eating something that has been handled by an infected person. Symptoms include watery diarrhoea, often with blood in the faeces, nausea and vomiting, stomach pains and fever. While the medieval man was probably more resistant to it than we are today, it could still be fatal. Even if it wasn't, the man's ability to do his duty was severely affected. Many of the spearmen and archers would have been infested with worms. Colds and influenza would have been common. Malaria was then endemic throughout Europe but was more of a summer infliction, there being a lot less mosquitoes around in the winter. On top of the health hazards, manning siege lines was boring and gave few opportunities for acquiring glory or loot. There was a steady trickle of desertion by archers and spearmen, while many of the knights found excuses to return to England to sort out a land dispute or see to a son's marriage. There was also a problem with the horses, which started to die off from, according to the chroniclers, the cold. As horses grow a substantial winter coat and are very capable of surviving all but the most severe weather, this may have been an epidemic of strangles[*], or it may have been

---

[*] A highly infectious respiratory disease of horses caused by the bacterium Streptococcus Equi. Even today it is often fatal and it spreads with incredible speed in large horse populations. Even if a horse recovers (unlikely in 1346/47), it can still be a carrier and never returns to its previous form.

starvation: hay would have been running out and barley and rye intended for the horses may have been eaten by the men.

In February 1347, commissions of array were issued for another 3,600 archers and the commissioners in Wales were instructed to provide more spearmen. These reinforcements were needed not only to make up the shortfall brought about by sickness, desertion and leave, but also to replace a contingent that had been sent off to Brittany with Sir Thomas Dagworth who had served there in the previous year with a small mobile force. There he had managed to distract the French from their sieges of the English garrisons of Brest, Lesneven and La Roche-Derrien. In a series of battles where his tiny band of men-at-arms and archers had seen off far more numerous French soldiers, he forced Charles of Blois to lift the sieges. Dagworth then joined the *Chevauchée* to Crécy before being sent back to Brittany in January 1347. Sir Thomas was typical of the professional soldiers who would make their reputations and fortunes out of this war. A younger son, born around 1306 of good but impoverished stock he started life as estate manager for the earl of Hereford and obviously impressed, for he married, far above his station, a granddaughter of Edward I. He was knighted, whether this was due to possible service in the Scottish wars of the 1330s or to the connections made by marriage is unknown. In 1345 he commanded a subunit under the Earl of Northampton in Brittany, where he did well and was appointed commander of English forces there when the earl returned to England in January 1346. In the next four years he would receive a large cash grant from Edward III, be ennobled, called to parliament and die fighting. A natural leader whose loyalty was unquestioned, he cared about his men, looked after them and made sure that any credit went to them. This had been unusual a commander at the time, but one that would become the norm as professionalism continued to permeate the English army.

The French had still not faced up to the implications of what they termed '*La Déconfiture de Crécy*', but Philip of Valois could not ignore the English army camped around Calais. Attempts to lift the siege by sea had proved futile so in early 1347 the French vassals were ordered to muster their troops at Amiens by

Whitsuntide (28 May in 1347). The troops did arrive, eventually, but it was not until July that the army was ready to move, and when they did Edward was understandably concerned. Although the summer weather had improved the health of his army there was still a large number on the sick list; long months in the siege lines had induced boredom and low morale; many soldiers had lost their physical fitness and fighting edge, and in June a reinforcement of the healthiest 100 men-at-arms and 400 archers had been sent off to Dagworth in Brittany.

Although this detachment weakened the Calais army it was a highly cost-effective investment. In Brittany Charles of Blois had reinstituted the siege of La Roche-Derrien, hoping that by so doing he could lure the English army into trying to lift the siege, when he could fight and win a battle on his terms. Instead it was the French who suffered a crushing defeat, for on 20 June 1347 Sir Thomas Dagworth led a night attack on the French army dispersed around its siege lines, and defeated it piecemeal. Sir Thomas himself was wounded and captured, escaped, captured again and escaped again, and when dawn broke on 21 June nearly half the French men-at-arms had been killed, and those nobles not killed had been captured, including Charles of Blois himself, whom Sir Thomas sold to the king for £3,500. At a stroke the whole balance of power in Brittany was reversed and the foundations laid for the eventual success of the Montfort faction in the Breton war of succession[*].

Meanwhile within Calais the siege was biting ever more sharply. The garrison had eaten all the horses and was starting on the cats and dogs, and so Jean de Vienne expelled another 400 citizens who were not contributing to the defence. This time Edward did not permit them to pass through his lines; he refused them food and water, and he let them die. Not everyone in the

---

[*] Often thought of as a separate war, the Wars of the Breton Succession were in fact campaigns of the Hundred Years War by surrogate, where England supported one faction for the throne of Brittany and the French another.

English camp agreed with this, but most did. By allowing the previous expellees to pass without hindrance the English had given de Vienne a pain-free way of extending the siege by reducing his ration strength, and there was also the question of spies and messengers being sent out in the guise of refugees. It was a hard decision, but the right one in the circumstances. With the approach of the French army from Amiens, summonses were sent to England to recall knights on furlough and those who had gone back to buy horses to replace those that had died during the winter. In any siege the investing army not only had to worry about sallies from the defenders, but also had to guard against the risk of being attacked from by behind by a relieving force. The French army got as far as Sangatte, saw that the English were apparently soundly entrenched and well able to withstand an attack (which they probably were, but not as well able as it appeared) issued a half-hearted challenge to come out and fight and then withdrew. The news of La Roche-Derrien had reached the army, the men were not enthusiastic after Crécy the previous year, and many saw no point in continuing the war. As they scuttled back to Amiens they were followed up by a mounted party led by the earls of Lancaster and Northampton who gave them no chance to rest or recover their appetite for a fight, and Philip now ordered his divisions to disband.

Inside Calais, Jean de Vienne had hung on in the hope of relief, and with the withdrawal of Philip's army that last chance was gone. A messenger was sent out offering to negotiate and Edward sent Sir Walter Manny in to parley. De Vienne said that he would surrender the town if the lives of the garrison and the property of the inhabitants were spared. Manny relayed the king's orders that in accordance with the customs of war at the time the lives of a garrison that held out during a siege were forfeit[*]. Only

---

[*] Not strictly true. Once a breach in the walls was created, if the garrison then refused to surrender and the town had to be taken by storm, with the probability of severe casualties to the attackers, then the garrison could be executed. This policy was implemented by Cromwell at Drogheda in

unconditional surrender was acceptable and Edward would do with soldiers and civilians as he wished. This policy was not popular with Edward's own knights, who pointed out that to kill men for doing their duty could rebound on them in the future. The whole point of adhering to modern laws of armed conflict that protect prisoners of war is to ensure that the other side does the same, and Manny and the others were arguing that very same point. Eventually, the king gave way and it was to de Vienne that the majority of the garrison and the civilians would be spared, but not their property, and six of the leading men of the town were to come to King Edward dressed only in their shirts and with nooses round their necks bearing the keys of the city. On the morning of 3 August 1347, Calais surrendered, and what happened next became the stuff of the French legend makers, desperate to produce some tale of heroism from the disastrous years of 1346 and 47.

The story goes that the six burgesses, led by Eustache de Saint Pierre who had supposedly volunteered for the job, came out of the city gates to find the whole English army drawn up on parade, with the king and his queen and senior officers seated on a platform. The emaciated party approached the platform and fell on their knees, and Saint Pierre asked for mercy. Edward refused and ordered them beheaded. At once there began a murmuring amongst the senior officers – to execute the men at once was bad enough, to execute them unshriven would be disgraceful. Edward was unmoved, and only when the pregnant queen, Philippa of Hainault, pleaded piteously with him was he moved to spare their lives. So is the account in French and English contemporaneous chronicles. The truth, almost certainly, is that this was a rehearsed charade to show the world that Edward was capable of great mercy. A queen might well argue with her husband in private, but never in public. Similarly, whatever advice the king's senior commanders might proffer in the council chamber, they would not cross him in the presence of a beaten enemy. Saint Pierre and his

---

1649 and one which Wellington said he wished he had enforced at Ciudad Rodrigo in 1812.

companions were spared, and Rodin's sculpture of them, erected in 1889, still stands in Calais, while a copy is in Victoria Tower Gardens in London.

Jean de Vienne and the more prominent of the French knights were sent off to join the growing band of notables in the Tower. All the buildings of Calais and their contents were now to be the property of King Edward. Despite the insignificance of Calais as a trading port, it turned out to be stuffed with riches of all description, largely as the result of many years of piracy. Once the majority of the inhabitants had been expelled, with little more than what they stood up in, the spoils of victory were collected and doled out. It was said that there was not a woman in England who did not wear something taken from Calais. It was Edward's intention to keep Calais, but rather than rule it as part of English France it would become a colony, with English merchants and tradesmen encouraged to settle there permanently, with the promise of free housing and land. Calais remained English for another 211 years, until Tudor neglect and French guile lost it in Mary Tudor's reign.

Chapter Two – The Plague

King Edward's initial intention was to follow up the victories of
Crécy and Calais by another great *chevauchée*, which might end
the war once and for all. But, the army was tired after over a year
of constant campaigning and money was once again in short
supply, so when the inevitable approach for negotiations was made
through the offices of the French cardinals, Edward was prepared
to listen. Although a rich nation, the military disasters found
France short of cash to pay the army, and so a truce was
imperative. Messengers raced between Calais and Amiens to try
to get agreement. The English were, of course, in much the
stronger position. When a nine months truce was signed at the end
of September 1347, it left the English in possession of all that they
had gained and held.

The return home of the king and most of his army was greeted
with acclaim. Parliament agreed that the money was well spent
and the king's personal position was enormously strengthened by
his obvious prowess in battle. The taking of Calais and its
plantation by English settlers was seen as providing England with
an opportunity for trade and an entrance to Europe that did not
depend upon friendly Flemings. On Saint George's Day[*] 1348 the
king founded the Order of the Garter, a chivalric order to comprise
but twenty-six members to be a close companionship of those who
had proved themselves in battle. It was intended to promote King
Edward's court as one just as glorious as any of those in Europe.
The order was to be headed by the king and his successors, who
would choose the membership, and there were only two
stipulations: knights were not to fight each other and could not
leave the kingdom without the king's permission. Of the twenty-
six original members eighteen were definitely present at the Battle
of Crécy and the others had distinguished themselves in various
other ways. The order would have its chapel in Windsor Castle

---

[*] For those readers unfortunate enough not to have won first prize in the
lottery of life by being born British, Saint George's Day is 23 April

and would support a chantry of twelve priests and twenty-six 'poor knights', originally men who had been captured by the French and who had had to sell their estates to pay the ransom for their freedom. It was not the first such order of chivalry, there was already one in Hungary and one in Castile, but both are now long gone and in any case were not as exclusive as the Garter. There is much speculation as to the origin of the name, mostly centring round a garter supposedly dropped by the countess of Salisbury at a post-siege celebratory party at Calais and picked up by the king with the words '*Honi soit qui mal y pense*' which can be translated as 'evil to him who thinks evil'. There are, however, a number of candidates for the countess. It is unlikely to be Katherine Montagu, countess of Salisbury, as she would have been getting on for fifty in 1347; it just might be Joan, the daughter of the earl of Kent (executed by Queen Isabella's Mortimer after the usurpation of Edward II), who had a racy past [*]. Legend also cites a mysterious Alice of Salisbury who by some accounts was a mistress of the king and by others a victim of rape by the king. We shall never know, but a more likely, albeit mundane, explanation is that the badge of the order had to be something that could be worn over armour. The order might just as easily have been the

---

[*] Known sarcastically at the time as the Virgin of Kent because she wasn't, later prudery called her the Fair Maid of Kent. She married Sir Thomas Holland in 1340 when she was twelve and he twenty-six. The marriage was clandestine but lawful and was consummated. When Sir Thomas went off with the Teutonic Knights in late 1340 to fight the heathens in what is now Prussia her mother married her to William Montagu, son of the earl of Salisbury and later the second earl of Salisbury himself, which ceremony duly took place with much pomp. When Sir Thomas returned he appears not to have mentioned that the girl had been married to him and became the Montagu's steward. Only after the 1346/47 chevauchée when Holland had made his name and his fortune in the capture of Caen did he begin proceedings in the papal court to get his wife back, which he eventually succeeded in doing in 1349. They had five children before Holland died in 1360 after which, still only thirty-three, she married the Black Prince, and gave him a son, later Richard II. Quite a lass.

order of the armband, and that the motto can equally well be translated as 'shame on him who thinks badly of it', referring to Edward's claim to the French throne. Now (2023) the Garter is the oldest order of chivalry in the world and while the twelve priests did not survive the reformation the twenty-six knights live on. Retired service officers they are no longer necessarily poor, very few are knights and their appellation was changed by King William IV to the Military Knights of Windsor.

Europe was now struck by a catastrophe so appalling that it made any major military endeavour impossible until it had run its course. In 1344 an argument between a Moslem and a Christian which resulted in the death of the Moslem in the town of Kaffa, a Genoese outpost on the south east coast of the Crimea, escalated into intercommunal rioting. At this point the local Khan decided to get involved on the side of his co-religionists. The Christians withdrew behind the walls of the city which was then besieged by the Khan. The city was well provisioned and its walls were stout. It seemed that the citizens had simply to hold out until relief arrived or the Khan gave up and withdrew. At some stage soldiers of the besieging force began to die in a most unpleasant fashion from a disease hitherto unknown and which had probably originated somewhere in central Asia. While this not unnaturally perturbed the Khan, he thought he could use it to his advantage, and so he had several bodies of his dead soldiers catapulted over the walls into the city. Inside, the mysterious disease began to spread with astonishing speed and the surviving inhabitants decided that there was only one thing for it and that was to flee the city by ship. A number of them sailed across the Black Sea, through the Bosporus, through the Sea of Marmora and down the Dardanelles into the Mediterranean. After a stop in Sicily to re-provision, where the disease caught hold of the island's population, the refugees arrived at Marseilles sometime in the summer of 1347. From there it spread rapidly throughout Europe. From contemporary descriptions it was almost certainly bubonic plague, a virus spread by fleas that live on rats and mice. In the unhygienic conditions of the time it was almost impossible to prevent it spreading, particularly in towns where people lived close together and sanitation was poor, and the mortality rate was very high indeed. In August 1348 it arrived in England, either on a ship from Bordeaux carrying wine or one from the supply run to Calais, landing at Weymouth, from where it spread inexorably through Dorset, Somerset, Devon and then to London where it was first reported in November. The symptoms were swellings in the groin and the armpits, black blotches on the skin, a fever and death within four days. France, already reeling from military defeat and without a strong central administration, suffered appallingly. Crops went unharvested and fields untilled; fodder that would have gone to warhorses went to animals that were of greater agricultural value. Knights who found their incomes gone took to brigandage. As the population shrank so did state revenues, the currency was devalued and the court and government fled Paris, with Philip wandering around the borders of Normandy with a handful of clerks and personal servants. To many of the French this was God's punishment, although witchcraft and sorcerers of various hues were also blamed, as was the practice of blasphemy which was now to punished by the removal of the tongue for persistent offenders. Inevitably, the Jews came in for even more persecution than usual.

In England the effects were less, but still serious. The death rate was particularly high amongst the clergy, who, if they were doing their job properly, were in constant contact with victims, and in the dioceses of York and Lincoln 44% of the beneficed clergy died, while in Exeter, Winchester, Norwich and Ely it was 50%. For long it has been generally accepted that up to a third of the population died in that first visitation, which by 1350 had largely run its course and was now in Scotland, but some modern authorities think that it may have been much more than that. Dislocation was far less in England than in France, largely due to a more efficient central government that controlled the whole country, and a popular king, compared to various semi-independent feuding magnates and a failed and unpopular king. In England this first outbreak tended to hit the poor and undernourished, while the nobility, living in a (relatively) cleaner environment were less severely affected, unlike their counterparts in France where the queen, the Duchess of Normandy and the Chancellor all died, as did many of the aristocracy. With the reduction in the labour pool English agricultural workers were no longer tied to their lords and could demand higher wages. Various strictures emerged from Westminster exhorting labourers to claim no more than they had before the plague, and lords who paid over the odds were to be fined (the French took a rather different view and there labourers who would not work for the old rates were branded). While in France law and order and government did break down for a time, in England, despite rising crime and economic problems, the authorities never lost control and recent excavation of a so-called plague pit in East Smithfield, London, has revealed that far from being tipped higgledy piggledy into a hole in the manner of Belsen, the bodies were buried in neat rows, each body in its own grave, albeit not in a coffin.

While neither side could embark on any large scale operations of war, the fighting did not die down completely. In 1349 there was an attempt to bribe a Genoese mercenary commander in Calais to leave the gate open and the drawbridge down one night to allow a French raiding party to recapture the town. The man took the money, agreed to betray the town on 31 December and sent a fast galley to report the bribe to King Edward. The king crossed to France with personal retainers and archers and ambushed the raiders as they crept through the gate. The Genoese kept the bribe. Then Philip persuaded the Castilians, who since the death of Joan Plantagenet had thought better of their alliance with the English, to send a fleet into the channel, presumably to disrupt the wine trade from Bordeaux, the supply convoys to Calais or both. English intelligence gave early warning and on 29 August 1350 off Winchelsea at the Battle of *Les Espagnols sur Mer* the English fleet, with King Edward, the Prince of Wales and the ten year old John of Gaunt aboard, won a great victory over a larger fleet of higher (and thus more difficult to board) Spanish ships. At the age of thirty-seven it was the last time Edward personally got involved in hand to hand fighting, but by now his prestige was such that he did not have to.

Then, in August 1350, just as France was recovering from the Black Death, Philip VI died to be succeeded by his thirty-one year old son, Jean II. Jean is known in French history as *Jean le Bel*, John the Good (or Fair), the myth makers having taken note of his undoubted personal courage and love of tournaments, while quietly ignoring that he was vicious, irrational, unjust, militarily incompetent and stupid (which in the pantheon of French royalty is very stupid indeed). He is described as being handsome and with a fine red beard, although in his portrait in the Louvre it looks more like designer stubble that has got out of control. He too founded an order of chivalry, the *Chevaliers de l'Etoile* whose members had to swear an oath never to leave a battle alive, which largely explains why the order no longer exists. What particularly annoyed the English, and reinforced the existing antipathy to the Papacy that would eventually find expression in the Reformation, was the creation by the Pope of twelve cardinals to mark the crowning – eight Frenchmen, three Spaniards and an Italian, completely ignoring the English candidates. Jean was in no position to renew the war just yet, although he did start to gather the funds for it, largely by even more oppressive taxation allied with debasing the currency - minting more of it while reducing the silver content. Despite the truce of Calais the skirmishing in Aquitaine and Brittany had never died down, and in Brittany on 20 July 1350 the great Sir Thomas Dagworth was treacherously ambushed and killed fighting furiously to the end. The following year Henry of Lancaster led a short but devastating *chevauchée* through Artois and Picardy, and in Brittany, the 'Battle of the Thirty' was perhaps one of the last hurrahs of chivalric warfare. A French force commanded by Jean de Beaumanoir sallied out of the castle of Josselin and arrived outside the walls of Ploermel eight miles away. Rather than undergo a siege the English garrison commander, Robert of Bambrough, agreed that thirty men-at-arms from each side would fight a decider on foot. Rules were agreed, to include which weapons could be used, and when there would be breaks for refreshment and the dressing of wounds, and the location was to be midway between the two castles. On 13 March

1351 the encounter duly took place, and the English lost (although they accused the French of cheating).

Dagworth's successor as theatre commander in Brittany was Sir Walter Bentley, a hard professional from a Staffordshire family that had often in the past been in opposition to, and in trouble with, the king. Edward III was not a man to hold grudges against those who could be useful to him and who were prepared to serve him loyally. He did not believe in the inheritance of the sins of the fathers is shown by the inclusion amongst his senior commanders of a Hugh Despenser and a Roger Mortimer, both sons of men whose execution Edward had ordered or had been associated with. On 14 August 1352 Bentley with a small force of perhaps only two hundred men-at-arms and three hundred archers beat a far larger French force at Mauron, midway between Rennes and Ploermel. In accordance with English tactical doctrine he placed his men on a slope with a hedge in front, men-at-arms on foot and archers on the flanks. The French had learned a little from Crécy and their commander, Guy de Nesle, ordered the majority his men to dismount while several hundred mounted men were ordered to ride down the English archers. Had the attack been properly coordinated and commanded it might have worked. As it was, the French mounted knights did disperse the archers on the English right, but instead of then wheeling round and attacking the English line in rear, they carried on to plunder Bentley's (sparse) baggage convoy. On the English left the archers repulsed the cavalry, but in doing so were unable to deliver the usual arrow storm on the advancing French infantry, and de Nesle did get his infantry line to close. The men having marched up hill in multi layered clothing under and over armour, however, were in no shape for pitched hand to hand fighting and were seen off by the English men-at-arms. As usual, casualties are hugely over or under stated. According to the chronicle of Geoffrey le Baker the French dead included ten great lords, 640 knights and noblemen and a number of 'common people not counted', while 140 knights and nobles were taken prisoner . A more recent source claims eighty nobles and 500 men-at-arms killed and 160 knights taken prisoner . The real figure is probably two hundred or so French killed (many of whom were knights of the Star) and the prisoner figure about right. Neither source makes any mention of English casualties, and yet there must have been some amongst the archers on the English right. Le Baker says that Bentley had twenty archers executed on the spot for running away when the French cavalry attacked, but this is most unlikely – although he may well have had one of the captains or vintenars executed as a warning to others.

Although England's economy had recovered more quickly from the plague than that of France (wages had gone up, but so had prices so the lords could retain almost the same income as before) Edward was quite happy to negotiate while still preparing for a renewal of the war. Desultory negotiations had been going on since the capture of Calais, but always foundered on Philip VI's refusal to restore the English lands other than as fiefs of the Valois, which was quite unacceptable to the English. Things changed by 1353, as not only had Philip been succeeded by Jean but Pope Clement VI had died and Innocent VI was elected to replace him. Innocent was even more pro French than his predecessor, but he did see the need to end the war in a Europe still trying to recover from the ravages of the plague. Serious deliberations began in the Castle of Guines, five miles south of Calais, which had been taken, in breach of the truce, by a *coup de main* led by John Dancaster, a squire of the Calais garrison who, bored by garrison duty, collected a few soldiers, took them over the Guines wall by night with blackened faces and seized the castle. The go-between, moving between Avignon, Paris and Guines was Cardinal Guy of Boulogne, and the result, arrived at in April 1354, was the Treaty of Guines by which in return for giving up his claim to the French throne Edward was to receive Aquitaine, Normandy, Touraine, Poitou and the town and surrounding area of Calais in full sovereignty. It would bring the war finally to an end, give the English what was rightfully theirs and allow Jean to retain part of his kingdom rather than lose all of it. The treaty was to be ratified by the Pope at Avignon.

It did not happen. Jean thought better of it, his magnates were against it and Guy of Boulogne was in any case out of favour. King Edward was angry and frustrated with the collapse of the negotiations, particularly as he had assured Parliament in Westminster that a permanent peace had been obtained and that there need no longer be increased taxation to support the war. King Jean must be made to see the error of his ways and this time there would be no compromise. The plan for 1355 was to attack France from three directions: the king himself would strike inland from Calais, Henry of Lancaster, now a duke, from Normandy, and the Black Prince (as the Prince of Wales was known after Crécy) from Aquitaine. There were problems with the weather and problems with finding enough soldiers, but in October 1355 King Edward landed at Calais with perhaps 8,000 men and moved inland towards Amiens where Jean of Valois had assembled a much greater French army. Then, bad news arrived from England: the Scots were on the rampage again, had invaded England on 6 November and were laying siege to Berwick Castle. They were perfectly accustomed to coping without a king (David was still a prisoner in England) and claimed that they were bound by treaty to attack England if France was invaded. When the Scots had last invaded in 1346 there were sufficient troops in the north to deal with them, but the need to raise three armies in 1355 and the reduction in the population caused by the plague, had forced the king to array men from the north, and there were very few left in the border counties. Edward had no choice but to reverse his progress into France, return to Calais and re-embark.

Lancaster's army never got to Brittany: constant bad weather and unseasonable winds kept blowing his fleet back to England's shores and the only English army that crossed the Channel and stayed was that of the Black Prince. Prince Edward landed in Bordeaux in September 1355 with perhaps 1000 men-at-arms, 1700 archers and a few hundred Welsh spearmen. Now aged twenty-five he had proved his personal bravery at Crécy but had never previously been in independent command. His father had, however, provided him with seasoned and wise officers to assist him. The earls of Warwick, Suffolk and Salisbury had all served in the Scottish wars, at Crécy and at the siege of Calais. They would provide advice when needed and curb any tendency to hot-headed adventurism. At Bordeaux the English were joined by their Gascon troops and having unloaded his horses and allowed his men time to recover from sea sickness the prince moved off on a chevauchée through Armagnac and Languedoc. He burned, he killed, he looted, he levelled and by November he had reached the Golfe de Lion, having traversed 300 miles from coast to coast. So far he had avoided fortified towns and castles; while tempted by Toulouse he bypassed it, and when he came under a bombardment from French trebuchets at Narbonne and it was apparent that the garrison was a strong one, he wisely withdrew, burning the suburbs as he went. Now it was time to turn about and return to friendly territory – the nights were drawing in, the rivers were rising and a large number of horses had been cast having been ridden too hard on inadequate feed. French troops were also on the move, as were private adventurers who sniped at the baggage train, heavy with a month's worth of loot. To return to Aquitaine meant crossing a series of rivers, now swollen with the rains and with bridges broken down by the French, but to the amazement of the latter the English did cross the rivers – the Ariège and the Garonne were supposed to be impossible to cross with horses – and struggled on westwards. Soon the pursuing French forces were only a day's march behind, and at night the English could see their enemy's camp fires. But the French too were held up by flooded rivers and dissension amongst the commanders as they argued about what to do next, and on 28 November 1355 the Black Prince and his army crossed the border into Aquitaine.

In some ways 1355 had been a disappointing year: the expected perpetual peace had not arrived, the three pronged attack had not happened, and the Scots had once more invaded England. The latter threat was soon dealt with, however, and while the Black Prince's mounted raid led to no great battles, it once again demonstrated the inability of the French king to protect his subjects, put heart into the Gascons, reduced the taxes that could be raised from the raided areas and liberated a great deal of valuable plate, cloth and wine, to say nothing of horses and prisoners for ransom. Edward's troops had good reason to be satisfied and they looked forward to a repeat the following year. Although they did not know it at the time, 1356 would see the second of the great English victories on land of the Hundred Years War.

The Black Prince spent the winter and spring of 1355/1356 in consolidating his position in Aquitaine and preparing for another chevauchée. Although no major operations were launched there were constant and limited raids into French territory designed to recapture English possessions and by the spring of 1356 thirty castles and towns had been recovered and garrisons installed. Orders were sent to England for the despatch of reinforcements and Sir Richard de Stafford was instructed to enlist 300 mounted archers. Two hundred were to be from Cheshire and the rest from wherever they could be found. They were to be arrayed, tested and equipped and conveyed to Plymouth to take ship for Bordeaux without delay and in any case by Palm Sunday (15 March 1356). A resupply of weapons was also needed and the Prince sent one of his logisticians, Robert Pipot of Brookford, back to England to purchase one thousand bows, two thousand sheaves of arrows (yet more featherless geese)[*] and 400 gross (57,600) bowstrings. Clearly the wastage rate of bowstrings was considerable, but Pipot had problems in getting arrows as all available stocks had already been bought up by the king, and fletchers had to be hired to work night and day to make the quantities needed. There was no problem in persuading soldiers to enlist provided that they were available, for the depredations of the plague were of course still a major factor. Pay was reasonable and the rules for the division of plunder and ransom clearly spelled out. Wages were calculated by the day and there was usually a generous advance of pay on enlistment. Captains and leaders of companies were paid a regard of 100 marks (about £66.66) per quarter for every thirty men they produced in addition to their own pay, and a leader who could

---

[*] A sheaf was twenty four arrows. Each arrow required two feathers, pinion feathers from a goose. A goose has four pinion feathers, two each side, and geese moult once a year. One goose could therefore provide the feathers for two arrows a year. For the latest demand therefore the feathers of 24,000 geese would be required. There were an awful lot of geese in England!

produce a hundred men (and there were some) could amass a lot of money in a reasonably short period of time, to say nothing of his cut of the loot and any ransoms paid for men captured by his company.

From the English point of view it was increasingly important to meet the main French royal army and defeat it. Despite the successes of the 1355 campaign and the enormous plunder that had been realised from it, the English were still no nearer to forcing the French to recognise the legitimacy of English France. A decisive battle was needed, one that would engage the main French royal army, defeat it utterly and end the war. Once again the English plan was to coordinate attacks into central France from three directions: Henry of Lancaster from Normandy, King Edward from Calais and the Black Prince from Aquitaine who would strike north for Paris and, while we have no written evidence, was almost certainly aiming to link up with Lancaster somewhere around the River Loire. The expense of such a plan, keeping three armies in the field, maintaining the various scattered garrisons and providing for the defence of Calais and Aquitaine, was enormous – around £100,000 in the financial year 1355/56 alone, about half for the Black Prince's forces – but England could afford it, partially from taxation but mainly from customs duties and profits accrued from the campaigns so far and the ransoms obtained.

Jean of France had huge problems. His policy of avoiding pitched battles until the English ran out of money and went home had failed completely; he had demonstrably failed to protect those whom he regarded as his subjects; his government was riven with dissent and still suffering from the dislocation caused by the plague; his son and heir was plotting against him with the king of Navarre, and he was very short of money with which to continue the war, so much so that he declared a moratorium on the payment of government debt, which ruined great man and humble tradesman alike. This latter was perhaps Prince Edward's major achievement of the previous year, for in a great swath of territory from Bordeaux to the Mediterranean sea the economy had been utterly ruined – it was calculated that by the destruction of

Carcassonne and Limoux (modern Limoges) alone the French had been deprived of the funds to support 1000 men-at-arms . English propaganda made much of Jean's inability to prevent the English from going wherever they wanted, of his profligate frittering away of funds and oppressive taxation, and stressing how much better life would be under the legitimate king of France – Edward III of England. The only solution short of surrendering to all the English demands – which would have cost him his throne and possibly his life from disgruntled French magnates – was to abandon previous strategy and bring the English to battle, preferably on terms favourable to the French.   Orders went out for men to be conscripted and mustered at various points along the River Loire.

On 4 August 1356 the Black Prince struck north towards Paris. As he could not afford to let a French army take advantage of his absence to invade Aquitaine, the seneschal, John de Chiverston, was left behind with a large force of about 2000 men, leaving Prince Edward with a total of around 5,000, three thousand archers and two thousand men-at-arms with a few hobilars. The whole army was mounted: they would move fast, never stopping long enough for the French to catch them at a disadvantage and only offering battle when it suited them to do so.   As in previous *chevauchée* no attention was paid to strongly fortified or defended castles or towns, but those that were only lightly held, or where the walls had fallen into disrepair, were swiftly taken and their stocks of food and wine taken to replenish the army. The baggage train was minimal and largely for carrying plunder and spare arrows and weapons – the army would live off the country and was covering around ten miles a day until the end of August when Edward's troops reached Vierzon on the River Cher, which town was found abandoned. The usual looting and burning in a wide area round about took place, and a detachment of troops under Sir James Audley and Sir John Chandos was sent off to do the same at Aubigny, twenty-five miles to the north east.   Audley and Chandos were, like Manny, Holland and Dagworth, men of relatively modest origins who rose in wealth and status from their prowess in war. Audley, around thirty-eight years old in 1356 was the illegitimate son of an Oxfordshire knight and a knight's daughter and is first mentioned by the chroniclers as being in the retinue of Edward Prince of Wales during King Edward III's expedition of 1346/47. He was present at Crécy and at the siege of Calais and while we do not know when he was knighted, he was one of the founder members of the Order of the Garter. John Chandos was a younger son of a Derbyshire knight and while his date of birth is unknown he was probably around the same age as Audley, for they appear to have been great friends and comrades in arms. Chandos was knighted in 1339 largely as a result of favourable comment as to his courage and ability in a single combat outside Cambrai; he fought at the sea battle of Sluys and, like Audley, was in the Prince of Wales's retinue at Crécy. He was on board the Prince's ship at Winchelsea in 1350 and, again like Audley, was a founder member of the Garter.

Audley and Chandos completed their work of destruction at Aubigny, and on their way back ran into and routed a band of French freebooters commanded by one Phillip de Chambry, known to his friends as *Gris Mouton*, or grey sheep, presumably from his appearance. It was from prisoners captured in this skirmish that the Black Prince discovered that the French were not as far away as he had thought. By now Jean of France had assembled an army and had moved the various contingents to Chartres, but had still no definite idea where the English were. With the obvious clue of a fifty mile wide trail of devastation pointing towards Paris, and hordes of refugees fleeing the invaders, Jean knew from which direction the Black Prince was advancing, but had no real idea of exactly how far he had got. What was clear to the French was that once the English crossed the Loire, assuming they could cross it, then the advantage would swing towards the French as the river was in spate and the French would hope to be able to trap the English army against it where they had no escape route.

Chapter Three – To Capture a King

It was probably around Vierzon that the Black Prince realised that any intention of joining up with the Duke of Lancaster must be abandoned. The duke had presumably calculated that if he continued in the direction of Tours he was going to meet the French army before he could join with Prince Edward. As he had no intention of fighting a hopeless battle he wisely withdrew, sending a message to the French king that he had no intention of fighting as the French hoped, but would 'go where he liked and do as he wished'. The Black Prince's expedition was not dependent on combining with Lancaster, but now that such was no longer possible Edward had to reappraise the situation. He was not afraid of a pitched battle with the French – indeed he hoped for it – but without the addition of Lancaster's troops to push further towards Paris would be unwise. It was essential that if a battle were to take place it must be on ground of Edward's choosing, where the English tactics could be best employed, rather than an opportunistic encounter battle dictated by the French. To move back the way he had come was not an option – that territory had been laid waste and there would be no supplies or fodder for the horses to be found. He decided to move west as far as Tours, from where he had the option of retiring south out of the devastated area and back to Bordeaux if no opportunity for a decisive battle presented itself.

It has to be said that Edward showed a great deal of confidence in himself and his men, and very little sense of urgency, reinforcing the evidence that he wanted to provoke a battle. He calculated that his mounted army could easily outmarch the generally ponderous French military machine. Hence, he moved along the River Cher to Romorantin, on the Loire, and laid siege to it. Not only could the Black Prince not afford to leave a hostile garrison in his rear, but there was also the hope that the French might try to relieve the town and thus give the Prince his battle. If Jean did not take the bait, however, Edward was confident that he could take the town and be on his way long before the French could interfere. Romorantin took five days to subdue, eventually forced to surrender when the walls were collapsed by mining and the central keep was set on fire, but there was no attempt by the French to raise the siege. More time was lost trying to find a crossing of the Loire in the Tours area, although the wait here may also have been dictated by a hope that the Duke of Lancaster might yet be able to rendezvous with the Prince. The French had destroyed all the bridges over the Loire from Tours north east to Blois and, having failed to find either the Duke of Lancaster or a crossing point, the Prince decided on 11 September to move south in the direction of the English base at Bordeaux, still at a leisurely pace. Whether this was due to overconfidence or because he deliberately wanted to entice the French into following him is still debated; all the evidence seems to point to the latter – but it may well have been a combination of the two. In fact the French army was much closer than either the Black Prince or Jean of France knew and soon they were marching parallel to each other as the English reached Chatelleraut and the French La Haye, twelve miles to the north east. Both sides were 'Anxious for battle for the sake of the peace which usually follows' as the chronicler Le Baker avers, and King Jean because he could no longer placate his own people by procrastination. Moving faster than anyone expected, on 15 September the French reached the east bank of the River Vienne at Chauvigny, from where they intended to move west towards Poitiers and cut the English off from Bordeaux. Reports from the Black Prince's mounted reconnaissance patrols that the French were now to their south discomfited Edward not one whit. The French had now committed themselves to battle and Edward would oblige them. The English baggage train and its accumulated booty was moved off to the west so as not to hinder the movement of the army.

On 17 September the first blows were struck when strong English mounted patrols under the Gascon knights d'Aubricourt and de Ghistelles intercepted the French rearguard, with the advantage to the English. The lead scouts of the main bodies clashed briefly too, when the English tried to intercept the French as they crossed the Vienne, arriving too late to do so. The French army now took up position on the plateau south east of Poitiers with Jean himself in the town and the English army to the south. Before first light on the following day, Sunday, the English army was on the march north, in order to find a position suitable for a battle, halting somewhere in the area of Nouille-Maupertuis, about four miles south east of Poitiers. The rest of the day was spent in negotiation on the instigation of the Cardinal of Périgord who scurried hither and thither trying to persuade each combatant to come to an arrangement that would avoid a battle. Eventually Edward agreed to talk and discussions began. On the French side were two archbishops, the count of Tancarville (captured at Caen and ransomed for £6,000) and three lords, while the English were represented by the earls of Warwick and Suffolk, senior commanders, and the trio of Audley, Chandos and Sir Bartholomew Burghersh. Burghersh was another who had made his name from war, although starting from rather more comfortable circumstances than most. He was the great nephew of Lord Baddlesmere, whose wife had refused Queen Isabella entry to Leeds Castle in 1322. The family lost their estates as a result, but regaining them after Isabella and Mortimer's invasion. They lost them briefly on Edward III's coup before finally establishing themselves in good standing. Burghersh's father, the first lord Burghersh, had made a great deal of money (relatively honestly) but Bartholomew owed his position to being a first class soldier who was present at most of Edward III's and the Black Prince's battles. He was another founding member of the Order of the Garter.

It is difficult to see what either side thought could come out of these parleys, or indeed whether they seriously wanted them to succeed. Points at issue included the prisoners in English hands and the obvious sticking points were the French demand that the English should provide hostages, and the English insistence that any agreement arrived at must be ratified by Edward III. Neither condition was in the least acceptable and when the French suggested that the question might be settled by a combat between 100 knights on each side, the earl of Warwick refused. He claimed the issue must depend upon a battle between two armies and nothing else. Even if the French could be trusted to keep their word the English had no intention of abrogating their tactical mix of archers and dismounted men-at-arms, which they knew gave them an advantage, in favour of an equal contest which they might lose. Jean was still leaning towards compromise but was eventually dissuaded by the rhetoric of two men, William Douglas and the Bishop of Challons. William Douglas commanded a force of 200 Scottish soldiers in the French army. There is some confusion as to exactly who this Douglas was – the Scots have lamentably few surnames and use but a handful of Christian names. He was not the William Douglas Lord of Liddlesdale who was now languishing in the Tower, but he certainly fought the English. He assured Jean that whatever the Black Prince might appear to agree to, he would continue to lay waste French lands and it would be much better to deal with him now than to have to fight him later in less advantageous circumstances. The Bishop made an impassioned plea, citing the shame and disgrace that the English operations had brought upon the present French king and his father. He insisted that the English were short of supplies, cut off from their base and hugely outnumbered. The only thing the English – any English – understood was force. Now was the time to deal with them once and for all. Jean was convinced and negotiations were broken off, the departure of the Cardinal's entourage to fight for the French only serving to emphasise the existing English suspicion of papal peacemakers. One advantage to the French was that they had bought time for a reinforcement of another 1000 men-at-arms to arrive. Perhaps buying time was the sole French intent in the first place.

While the negotiations were going on throughout the Sunday the English were preparing their position. In conformity with what was now standard tactical practice the three divisions would dismount and take position with two forward and one in rear, with archers on both flanks. We are told that the Vanguard was commanded by the earls of Warwick and Oxford, the second division by the Prince himself, and the rearguard by the earls of Salisbury and Suffolk. Confusingly, the Prince took up position in rear, as was normal procedure for the overall commander. He had the vanguard on the left and rearguard on the right covering the front. Command arrangements for the Vanguard and Rearguard are on the face of it unclear. Divided command is never a good idea and was a major factor in the series of defeats suffered by the French for most of the war. The chroniclers were not, of course, military men and it may be that they simply tell us the senior magnates in each division, rather than implying that they exercised command jointly. While joint command might work in a static battle of attrition it would be a recipe for chaos once any form of manoeuvre was required. We may assume that divisions were commanded by the senior magnate in each (in this case Warwick and Salisbury). While not all historians agree the exact positions of the opposing armies, the most likely location for the eventual English defensive position is on a low ridge running along an ancient track across a bend on the River Miosson, on the Plaine de Plumet west of the village of Les Bordes. The frontage is about 800 yards and the flanks are protected by steep drops to the river, while the rear is protected by the river itself. French accounts say the French army marched along a '*maupertuis*', or 'bad road' from Poitiers to get there, and there is what is now a farm track running south south east from Gibauderie through Le Maupas and Brout de Chevre to La Cadrousse, which is of considerable antiquity and may well be the road referred to. The two forward battles were on the track, the right flank archers south of La Cadrousse and those on the left somewhere around Le Plan. The reserve would have been placed some hundred yards to the rear, with a small reserve of 200 mounted knights under the Gascon lord the Captal de Busch.

This was an excellent position for the English way of fighting. The flanks were secured by thick woods on one side and a steep escarpment on the other, and the frontal approach was crossed by sunken lanes and thick hedges. If the Anglo-Gascon army had around 2000 men at arms and 3000 archers, and the three divisions were of roughly equal size, then the frontage to be covered, around 800 yards, would dictate that the forward divisions took post in no more than three ranks. Each division of archers would, as usual, have formed up in a square, lozenge or wedge shape. The Black

Prince was not concerned about fighting a battle, even against a far larger force of probably around 3,000 crossbowmen and 16,000 men at arms, but he was concerned that the French might play for a stand off until the meagre rations carried by the English ran out, and the Prince would be forced to march off to find resupplies. Of course the Prince could decide to attack the French, but to do so against such superior numbers and where the English missile weapon could not be used to best advantage would be to invite disaster. It was imperative that the French be encouraged to attack, but they were unlikely to do so if they thought the English were well ensconced in their favourite defensive posture – the French had learned at least that from Crécy. The French would however be likely to attack if they thought they could catch the English on the line of march, or retreating, and it appears that Edward ordered his own division and that of Salisbury on the right flank to manoeuvre in order to give the impression that they were departing.

For all his many faults Jean was inclined by now to listen to sound advice. Many of his senior commanders had faced the English, if not at Crécy then in Normandy or Brittany, and Sir William Douglas had fought them in Scotland, and perhaps in France too. These men insisted that to send heavy cavalry against a dismounted English line was suicide: the only way to deal with English foot-soldiers whose flanks were secure was for the French to dismount too. They were also well aware of the slaughter that could be dealt out by English archers. The remedy was to attack them with cavalry, but only with men and horses that were covered in plate armour that arrows would not pierce. Mindful of this very sound advice Jean had ordered 500 knights to equip their horses with armour that covered the animals' bodies, head and necks completely. It would slow them down, but it would allow them to reach the hated archers and kill them. Apart from this mounted task force, split into two units each commanded by one of the French marshals, the French army was divided into three battles or divisions. The vanguard was commanded, at least in name, by the Dauphin[*] , Jean's son, the second division by Jean's brother the Duc d'Orleans and the third by Jean himself with the bearer of the oriflamme – signifying no quarter or mercy – by his side. Despite the French having three or four times as many men as the English, the Black Prince had chosen his ground well and his numerical inferiority was partially nullified by the approach being restricted by marshes, streams and small ravines which limited the number of men that could advance at any one time.

The French plan, if they could not starve the Black Prince out, was to send the armoured cavalry against the archers, and having taken them out of the frame, to attack with the lead division on foot, supported by the next two divisions if they were needed, which they surely would not be. The hedges and trees made it difficult to see exactly what the English were up to. The commander of the right half of the anti-archer cavalry task force, Marshal Arnoud Audrehem, encouraged by William Douglas, probably stationed around the east side of the Grand Chene forest, was convinced that he could see movement of pennants and banners in the left hand English division of the earl of Warwick. Perhaps he could, this may have been Edward's planned encouragement – and without reference to anyone ordered his men to charge. Up the slope they came and at first the volleys of arrows had little effect, glancing off the plate armour of man and horse. This would have had very serious repercussions had not Warwick's second-in-command, the earl of Oxford, not dismounted and run to the archers, shouting to them to move further to the flank and ordering them to shoot at the horses (unarmoured) legs. Now the tables were suddenly turned, as arrows sliced into horses' legs and bellies. Those animals not brought down but with arrows hanging off stifles and rumps became uncontrollable: they reared, whipped round and dumped even the most competent horsemen, before galloping back the way they had come and over unhorsed knights. Audrehem was

---

[*] Jean II's son, Charles, was the first to be styled Dauphin, henceforth the title of the heirs to the French throne. It came from the territory Dauphiné, embodied into France by his grandfather, Phillip of Valois.

captured and Douglas badly wounded, only evading capture (and probable execution) by being carted off the field by his personal retainers. It was a terrible slaughter of the pride of France's equines, only equalled by that which befell Marshal Jean de Clermont and the other mounted task force. He had not been fooled by the appearance of waving guidons, but when his brother marshal went charging off against the English left he had little choice but to follow suit against the right. Clermont was even more restricted than Audrehem for he came up against a thick hedge with only one carter's gap in it, wide enough for perhaps four horses abreast. Having run the gauntlet of the arrows he then came up against infantry at the gap. He too could make no progress, and the survivors fled, picking their way through downed horses and men. The first phase of the battle had gone in favour of the English, but their officers now had to ensure that their men stayed in position and resisted the temptation to chase and take prisoners.

Now it was the turn of the French dismounted men-at-arms. The first division, led by the eighteen year old Dauphin, who made up in personal courage what he lacked in common sense, advanced along the *maupertuis* preceded by a screen of crossbowmen. With a strength of around 5,000 men and covering an initial frontage of 1,000 yards or so they would presumably have been in four or even five ranks. They had to climb the slope and negotiate the hedges before they could get to grips with the English infantry. Soon the inevitable arrow storm began to strike home, disposing of the crossbow men and forcing the men-at-arms to crowd together towards the centre. It causing death and destruction to such an extent that one chronicler says that the division was destroyed by arrow fire. While this was probably an exaggeration, the effort of trudging uphill for eight hundred yards or so in plate armour (and the French knights were always more heavily armoured than their English equivalents) and then coming under attack from something like thirty thousand arrows each minute for the last three hundred yards or so, meant that when the Dauphin's men managed to force their way through the hedge and meet their opponents they were in no great shape for the physically punishing business of hand to hand fighting. They had prepared for such by shortening their lances, normally ten to fourteen feet in length and intended to be used on horseback, to a far more manageable five feet, which allowed them to compete on more even terms with the English wielders of pole arms, but it mattered little. Once two lines of men-at-arms closed it was question of who could thump the hardest: a sword would probably not go through plate armour or chain mail – although a halberd point might for the former and would for the latter – and the aim was to knock one's opponent off his feet when he could be despatched by a dagger though crevices in the armour or the visor slits – or be persuaded to yield on the promise of ransom. Try as they might the men of the Dauphin's division could not break the English line and as casualties were mounting the Dauphin (or more probably one of his professional 'advisers') ordered a withdrawal. Even in modern armies a withdrawal is one of the most difficult phases of war. Amongst inexperienced or undisciplined troops it can too often turn into a rout, and this is what happened here. The Dauphin himself was hastened off the field by his personal retainers – a French heir was far too valuable a prize to risk capture – while those of his defeated troops who could still move fell back upon the next division in a disorderly panic. The commander of the second division, Jean's brother the Duc d'Orleans, seeing the Dauphin being removed from the stage decided that he should depart as well, which he did, taking his two nephews, the Ducs d'Artois and Normandy, with him. The men of Orlean's division, seeing themselves deserted by their commander, not unnaturally saw no point in staying and in moments they too were transformed into a disorderly rabble. Some called for their horses to be brought forward to affect their escape, others ran into the woods, others fell back upon the Jean's third division, the only part of the army to stand its ground.

Jean did not run, and nor did his division, which was augmented by those of the first two divisions that had not fled the field and the crossbowmen who had survived the first French attack. Altogether this final French formation probably now numbered around 7,000 men, mostly men-at-arms, or considerably more than the Black Prince could muster. Furthermore, the men of Jean's division were mostly fresh, whereas the English and their Gascon allies had been in their battle positions for over twenty-four hours, exhausted, short of food and water and having taken casualties. Jean ordered his reserve to dismount and join the line, and the advance began with the French moving towards the by now depleted English lines with a screen of crossbowmen in front. The archers were by this time running very short of arrows and the Knighton chronicle tells us that they ran out into no-man's-land to pull arrows from corpses and the wounded to be used again, and that the real pessimists amongst them armed themselves with stones to throw at the advancing enemy. The Black Prince was well aware that while so far the fortunes of battle had been with him, the tide could easily turn and he could still suffer a massive defeat. He ordered the Gascon Captal de Busch to take his mounted reserve and a party of mounted archers (perhaps fifty or sixty) to work his way round to the flank and attack the French from the rear. Meanwhile, the French crossbowmen and the English archers began a long range duel, which was won by the archers, despite their shortage of ammunition. The crossbowmen disposed of, the archers turned to the advancing infantry, but while the high angle arrow storm wreaked its usual carnage, the French in the front two ranks were relatively unscathed as they advanced behind their interlocked and angled upwards shields. The Captal and his party now began to move back prior to working their way round to the French rear, and this seemed to some of Edward's troops as the beginning of a retreat. Some murmuring began and Edward, fearful that panic might set in and infect the whole of his division immediately ordered 'Banners – Advance'. While this stilled any notion of a withdrawal, it was a very risky move. Standing on the defensive with hedges and other obstacles to their front and with archers on the flanks the English were in a reasonably secure posture, whereas to advance gave up the advantage of ground and gave the French the ability to use their superiority in numbers. The Prince's division moved forward, at first level with and on the left of Warwick's division, and then ahead of it until the two lines of infantry met with a mighty roar of

'*Saint Denis*' and '*Beate Martin*'[*] from the French and 'God and St George'[†] from the English . Now was the crunch for the Black Prince: the French line lapped round his, the English missile weapon could not be used and it now came down to bloody brute strength, with the archers picking up discarded lances and swords from the first French assaults and joining in where they could. The French pushed the English back: Poitiers was going to be a French victory after all. And then, just as suddenly, the tide turned again. The earl of Salisbury turned his troops to their right and led them north, advanced them into line and fell upon the French left flank. At the same time the Captal de Busch's archers, having worked round to the west, appeared on the *maupertuis* and began to shoot arrows into the backs of the French men-at-arms, only pausing to let the Captal and his mounted followers hammer into the French rear. Disciplined infantry in line can withstand cavalry if their flanks are secure, but not if that attack is preceded by an arrow storm and not of it comes from a totally unexpected direction and not if they are already being assaulted from two other directions at the same time. Faced with the Black Prince in Front, Warwick's very nasty infantry to their left and archers and cavalry to their rear, Jean's division began to fall apart, with formations broken banners began to fall and men were running out of the line to escape or find their horses, being promptly cut down by lightly armed archers hovering on the flanks. In minutes the battle was over and the slaughter of those not worth holding for ransom began. Those who could fled towards what they thought would be the safety of the city of Poitiers, but found the gates closed against them, many being killed by the pursuing Captal and his mounted knights. Jean II was captured with his youngest son Philip, as were

---

[*] It is said that the English Cockney slang expression 'All my eye and Betty Martin', meaning incomprehensible rubbish, comes from what the English thought the French '*Aidez moi beate Martin*' to be.

[†] Although if the Black Prince's soldiers were anything like their modern descendants, they were probably shouting something very different.

four royal princes (including the Count of Tancarville, who was by now making a habit of being captured by the English), eight counts, around 2,000 lesser nobility, the Archbishop of Sens and twenty senior clergy. This latter was yet more evidence, thought the English, of Papal bias, for as the contemporary satirical verse had it:

> Now is the Pope a Frenchman born
> And Christ an Englishman
> And the world shall see what the Pope can do
> More than his saviour can

Those French slain included two dukes, one marshal, one Constable of France, several pages from the French equivalent of Burke's peerage, the bearer of the oriflamme and the Bishop of Challons, the most vociferous exponent of fighting a battle on that day. Altogether the French probably lost around 2,500 dead, and although a total of perhaps 5,000 casualties may not seem very much it was who they were that was significant, for at a stroke the government and the administration of the French nation had been rendered impotent – dead or prisoners of war. Not only was it a massive tactical victory for the English, it was a huge strategic victory too, one that might well bring the war to an end. English losses were slight, perhaps surprisingly, and were probably no more than a few hundred dead and wounded although amongst the latter was Sir James Audley, carried in on a shield, stripped of his armour and laid on a bed in the Prince's tent. While in attendance on the Prince when Edward's division was in rear, he asked permission to join the battle and dashed off into the thick of the fighting. It was thoroughly irresponsible, but the sort of behaviour that appealed to the Black Prince (and indeed to well-bred society generally) and as a result of which Audley was granted an annual pension of £300 (around sixteen years' salary for a man-at-arms).

The capture of Jean was of course a tremendous coup, and there was much argument as to who had captured him, for while he would have to become the Black Prince's prisoner, his actual captor would be well rewarded. It seems that Jean, realising that the game was up, looked around the field to see where the Black Prince was, as it was to him that a king should surrender. Edward was not in the vicinity and it may have been a renegade French knight in the English service to whom Jean yielded. In any event it was not until the arrival of the earl of Warwick that the unseemly argument going on around Jean was stilled, and Warwick took charge of the royal prisoner and took him to the Prince.

Edward's Anglo-Gascon army camped that night in the Forest of Noailles to the east of the field of battle, the baggage train was called forward and tents erected for the Prince and his immediate retinue, where he entertained Jean, his son and the senior French prisoners to supper – the food sequestered from the French stores, as the English had none. Gentlemen may fight each other, but they do not have to hate each other, and the Black Prince assured Jean that his father, Edward III, would treat Jean as befitted his high born status (although continuing to refer to him as 'the usurper'). It was not until the next day that the English could count the French dead, many of whom had already been robbed and stripped by the locals. The bodies of around 150 of the highest-born were taken away by the clergy of Poitiers and buried in the Dominican church or the Franciscan cemetery, while the rest were left where they lay, to be eventually loaded on carts and dumped in grave pits near the church. It was now time for Edward and his army to head back to the safety of Aquitaine, and while the Prince had inflicted a massive defeat on the French he could not assume that he was safe from them. Poitiers contained a large garrison and was far too well fortified to fall quickly; the Dauphin was still on the loose and might act as a rallying point, while although the division of the Duc d'Orleans had fled the field it had done so without casualties, and was probably still somewhere in the vicinity. Given stout leadership the French might yet block the route to Bordeaux and pluck a victory of sorts from the ashes of defeat. Speed was of the essence but movement would be slowed in any case by the baggage train, where the booty had been hugely increased by the rich arms and robes acquired from the battle. Add to this the huge flock of prisoners, most of them on foot, and the chances of getting to Bordeaux without interference were sharply reduced. The solution was to use captured horses to carry baggage and to release all but the most important of the prisoners, having first made them promise to report to Bordeaux and pay their agreed ransoms 'by Christmas'.

Chapter Four – After the Battle

The Black Prince's army marched straight to Bordeaux, a distance of 125 miles as the crow flies (but as the soldier does not walk). They averaged around fourteen miles a day and arrived at Bordeaux on 2 October 1356. Messengers were sent to England to give the good news to the King and the people, which was immediately ordered to be announced from all pulpits in the kingdom and read out at the market crosses. Coupled to this was more good news from Brittany, where the Duke of Lancaster was supporting John de Montfort in gobbling up towns loyal to Charles of Blois, who, released from prison on parole pending payment of an enormous ransom of around £60,000 and thus unable take up arms, could only watch as more and more of Brittany fell to the English. Eventually he fled to Paris to join the Dauphin in the Louvre.

In Bordeaux, Prince Edward and his men settled down to see the winter out until the spring weather would allow safe passage for the army to return to England. Some of the French noblemen who had promised to turn up with their ransom money defaulted. Even so, the money raised, along with the plunder acquired in the chevauchée, paid for the cost of the campaign many times over. The ransom for the Archbishop of Sens was paid – £8,000 – and King Edward bought a batch of nobles for £66,000, an outlay he would recoup with a handsome profit to boot. In London there was jubilation. In Paris dismay swiftly turned to anger. Their armies had been defeated, their king captured, and his brother and sons had run away. Knights who had escaped the slaughter dare not show their faces in Paris, and many could not even return home for fear of being blamed for the disgrace and physically attacked.

Negotiations now began from Bordeaux, before Jean and his court were taken to England. While Jean was prepared to concede almost anything for his freedom, the Estates General (nobility, clergy and bourgeoisie), nominally headed by the Dauphin, were trying to govern a kingdom that was rapidly falling apart. They did not regard the return of their king as their first priority, rather they wanted to find a way to end the war, either by raising an army big enough to expel the English, or by coming to terms with them. King Edward too, was in no hurry to release Jean, rather he saw him as a useful pawn in arriving at a permanent settlement. His secret instructions to the Prince of Wales in Bordeaux were to enter into negotiations but to stall and to agree to nothing except perhaps a temporary and short truce, which was in any case to exclude Normandy and Brittany. In Paris, the Dauphin suspended the Estates General and attempted to raise money by a further devaluation of the coinage. This aroused massive civil disobedience, and when no help could be obtained from the Francophile Holy Roman Emperor at a conference in Metz, the Dauphin's clique had no option but to recall the Estates and to concede to their demands for a root and branch reform of the administration. This was to include the dismissal and imprisonment of many of the Dauphin's and his father's advisers, the withdrawal of the new (devalued) coinage, an insistence that the Dauphin could only rule with the advice of a council nominated by the Estates, and a levy of new taxes to support a continuance of the war. No mention was made of raising money to release Jean. The Dauphin agreed to all the demands – being without a sou in his empty treasury he had no alternative. When the news percolated down to Bordeaux, Jean decided to take matters into his own hands and issued letters to be taken to Paris and read out at street corners repudiating the new administration and cancelling the levy. This resulted in even more chaos and a counter repudiation from the Dauphin, and when Jean entered into negotiations with the Prince of Wales nothing could be decided except for a two year truce to run until Easter 1359.

In the spring, ships arrived from England to bring the army home, and on 24 May 1357 the Black Prince and his army made a triumphal entry into London to the cheers of the populace. Jean rode on a smart grey charger, while the Black Prince rode a modest pony – no doubt to make the point that for all the French bombast and show, it could avail nothing against English skill at arms. Jean was lodged in the Palace of Savoy, built by Henry of Lancaster with the proceeds of French ransoms and near what is now the

Savoy hotel in the Strand, and began a luxurious detention while negotiations continued for his ransom. Edward III took a liking to his captive and took him hunting at Windsor, and occasionally paraded him along with that other captive king, David II of Scotland, now in his eleventh year in the Tower.

In June 1357, the French deputation arrived at Westminster to attend what would be a long drawn out conference to decide upon terms to bring the war to an end. It was headed by Cardinals Périgord, who was regarded with great suspicion by the English, and Cappoci, an Italian who was considered to be relatively unbiased. With them was a whole plethora of lawyers, civil servants, advisers, royal councillors and general hangers-on, all with their own servants, and who had to be accommodated and fed. Parallel to these talks were discussions with the Scots, who had finally realised the hopelessness of continuing hostility to England when their backers, the French, were in such dire straits. At a meeting in Edinburgh they agreed to pay a ransom of £67,000 – a huge sum for an impoverished country with a small population and no raw materials – to be paid over ten years, during which time the Scots agreed not to take up arms against England and to provide hostages against good behaviour. King David was brought up to Berwick to attend the signing in October and was then released, although he now had little authority over the quarrelling factions in his country. Meanwhile after much discussion and argument as to the agenda, a draft treaty between England and France was at last agreed to in December 1357. It allowed for almost a third of French territory, including Calais and the pale around it, to be ceded to Edward III in full sovereignty and a ransom of £650,000 with £100,000 down, after which Jean would be released on parole subject to hostages being delivered. In return, Edward would give up his claim to the throne of France.

The English parliament was summoned to meet at Westminster in February 1358 to agree the terms of the treaty. The members were in no hurry to come to a conclusion. England was now safe from invasion but there were vested interests in continuing the war: the professional soldiers, civil servants who would administer conquered areas, owners of troopships hired by the government, manufacturers of arms and armour, bowyers and fletchers and, presumably, the owners of flocks of geese. Parliament decided that a solution to other longstanding matters could be tacked onto the treaty, particularly matters of papal authority. The pope was known to want peace between England and France so concessions could be squeezed from him in order to get it. Specific matters were the taxation of English clergy by the pope, which meant English money going to Avignon in France, and appointments by the pope to English ecclesiastic posts, which most Englishmen felt should be a matter for them and not for some foreigner across the seas. Similar grievances would eventually lead to a final break with the Roman church less than two centuries later. An embassy to Avignon would mean sending at least one senior bishop, lawyers, civil servants, clerks and escorts and would take a very long time, while armies would continue to be paid and arms manufacturers continue to thrive. King Edward drew the line at this, and while he agreed that emissaries could be sent to Avignon, they could be reduced to a couple of knights and a clerk or two and thus conclude their business promptly. At the same time, Jean, recognizing that the terms of the treaty might not be universally favourable in France, arranged a group of his advisers to explain the finer points to government and people.

The difficulty for Jean was that France was effectively in a state of civil war. The Estates trying to govern without their king attempted to collect the increased taxes. But, with the death or capture of so many magnates, normally the enforcers of good order and discipline, lawlessness spread. Demobilised soldiers and deserters, mainly English and Gascon but some Frenchmen too, formed themselves into 'free companies', or routiers, and roamed the countryside working for whoever could pay them. If no paymaster could be found they simply appropriated a suitable castle or fortified town and set themselves up as district robber barons, levying tolls on all who moved and taxes on those who did not. The king of Navarre, who had been imprisoned by Jean for plotting against him, escaped from prison and arriving in Paris 'persuaded' the Dauphin to pardon him. In Paris, the third estate, that of the bourgeoisie, was increasing in influence due to the loss of authority of the nobility. Their leader, a prosperous cloth merchant by the name of Etienne Marcel, defeated and disgraced at Poitiers, considered at one point making Charles of Navarre (who was, after all, a Capet) king of France. Navarre, who was quite happy to claim the crown when the time was ripe but was far too clever to have it given to him by acclamation of the mob, left Paris at speed, followed by the Dauphin in March 1358 who felt (rightly) that government had broken down to such an extent that even his life was in danger. This was finally brought home when agents of Etienne Marcel broke into the Dauphin's chambers and murdered two high ranking officials lodging with him. The Parisians were now in control of the capital and they were against any treaty with England.

In the French countryside those magnates still in control of their estates and having to raise money either for their own ransoms or those of their relatives, and for the eventual ransom of Jean II, began to put even more pressure on their tenants and peasants, already taxed almost to extinction. Finally, the worm turned. It began in the Beauvaisis (now the *departement de l'Oise*) in 1358 when the peasants, taxed and exploited beyond endurance, rose and attacked their masters with whatever weapons they could find. It appears to have been a spontaneous rising and in savagery it presaged the French revolution of four hundred years later, but unlike the latter did not have a corps of the middle classes and educated to lead it, at least not at first. The bloodshed and disruption caused by the *Jacquerie* (Jacques was then the commonest French Christian name amongst the peasantry) was horrific, mainly directed against the nobility, the clergy and any owners of property. Lynchings and burnings spread, and as the movement expanded into Champagne and Picardy the reports of their doings became more and more lurid. One tale circulating told of a lady being gang raped and then forced to eat the roasted flesh of her husband. At least they roasted him first. In the past there had been regular outbreaks of defiance of authority, sometimes with violence, but they had usually fizzled out in a few days with little harm done. Here, however, the peasants appear to have been so shocked by the excesses of what they had done that they had no option but to keep going, attracting some townsmen and minor nobles – who no doubt thought that by joining they could preserve their own lives and property. Etienne Marcel tried to make common cause with them, which did him no good in the end, while when a deputation of the *Jacquerie* tried to enlist the support of Charles of Navarre he turned his soldiers on them and slaughtered the lot.

While the *Jacquerie* were neither encouraged nor supported by Edward III (peasants massacring their betters were not to be approved off, even if the betters were French) their activities served his purpose in that it concentrated the minds of the French government and encouraged them to find a means of ending the war so that they could concentrate on restoring order internally. France was now in a state of complete and utter confusion, with the free companies, the Jacques, the Navarrese, the Dauphin and the citizens of Paris all in arms and all out for what they could get. What was increasingly clear was that the *Jacquerie* was a threat to any sort of established order and when Charles of Navarre and noblemen whose castles had not been stormed began to get organised the armies of peasants could not stand against them. Although destruction was immense – eighty castles and manors destroyed between Soissons and Paris alone – by mid-June the rebellion was over and retribution began, with the vengeful nobility meting out punishment every bit as unpleasant as that inflicted by the rebellious peasants. Their leaders were executed in novel ways, and the result of the rising, seen as threatening everyone's way of life (except of course that of the downtrodden peasantry), was an upsurge of loyalty to the crown in the shape of the Dauphin, a trickling away of Charles of Navarre's supporters and second thoughts by the citizens of Paris. The latter were beginning to turn against their *ci devant* leader, Etienne Marcel, who had made common cause with Charles against the Dauphin, and had allowed the detachments of the army of Navarre, mainly composed of English mercenaries, into the city. On 31 July the mob rose, in the name of the Dauphin, and murdered Etienne and his principal lieutenants. On 2 August the Dauphin entered Paris and Charles of Navarre withdrew his army from its encampment at St Denis, looted the abbey and then marched off to Mantes to plot his next moves.

Despite the pleadings of Jean's advisors, the terms of the treaty agreed at the Westminster conference were not agreed by the Dauphin and his government, their confidence restored by the departure of Navarre and the end of the Parisians attempt at independence. Edward received their refusals and decided that only another military campaign would bring the French to their senses. Accordingly, more claims were attached to those already in the treaty, including a restatement of the claim to the French crown, and an army, numbering 10,000 men (according to the Chandos Herald) but more likely 6,000. It was evenly split between men-at-arms and archers and landed at Calais on 28 October 1358. The army advanced through Artois and Champagne, burning, looting and levelling in the usual manner, as far as Rheims. One of the men-at-arms was the poet Geoffrey Chaucer, whose experiences led him to write later: 'there is ful many a man that crieth 'Werre! Werre!' that wot ful litel what werre amounteth.'* The army stayed at Rheims from December 1358 until January 1359, in appalling winter conditions, and having failed to force a surrender of that heavily fortified city, moved off to Paris. In accordance with the now standard English military practice Edward took up a defensive position and tried very hard to persuade the Dauphin to come out of the city and attack him. He even sent Sir Walter Manny up to the walls to shout insults at the craven French, some of whom were beginning to learn of the inadvisability of attacking an English army in a position of their choosing, and wisely resisted the offer. The only small crumb of comfort for the French at this time was a raid on Winchelsea in March 1360. A few French ships hove to off shore and landed men who burned the town, stayed there for one night and left again. The English had grown complacent; no such raid had happened in twenty years and the infliction on them of the sort

---

* In Middle English 'there are many men who cry for war without knowing what war amounts to'

51

of terror they had been imposing on the French for many years caused short lived panic and long lived indignation.

King Edward now moved off to Chartres, and began to lay waste the area round about. It was the realisation that the English could continue to wander all over France dealing out death and destruction at their leisure for as long as they liked provided they avoided fortified cities that brought the Dauphin and his advisers to their senses. Negotiations began at Brétigny, near Chartres, in May and in a week agreement was reached. The terms were very much the same as those in the December 1357 document, except that the ransom was reduced to £600,000. It was signed by the Dauphin for his father and the Black Prince for his at Calais in October 1360. King Edward was to have Aquitaine, Ponthieu and Calais in full sovereignty and would drop his claim to the French throne. Once two thirds of the ransom had been paid, raised by swingeing taxes on salt, wine, cloth and most movable goods and the betrothal of Jean's eleven year old daughter to the son of the Duke of Milan, Jean was allowed to return to France leaving his three younger sons behind. When John of Anjou broke his parole, returned to France and refused to come back, Jean went back to England in his son's stead, and was so well looked after that he died in the Savoy Palace in April 1364 still only in his mid-forties. Meanwhile the territory had been exchanged and the Black Prince, now duke of Aquitaine, installed as the ruler of English France. It seemed a very satisfactory outcome.

The Treaty of Brétigny marked the culmination of Edward III's twenty-four years of campaigning in France, and the end of the first phase of the Hundred Years War. The king had stated his claim to the French crown aged twenty-four and he was now forty-seven. Poitiers was a great victory and told the world, if the world needed telling, that the English had moved from being backward amateurs in the waging of war to being the foremost practitioners of it. The combination of professional soldiers fighting on foot with archers on the flanks was unbeatable, and the mobility of English armies meant that the French could neither trap them, nor fight them other than on ground which favoured the English, nor starve them out – although sometimes the latter was a close run thing. Certainly, the Black Prince had been unable to take Rheims or Paris in 1356, but he had accepted that fact rather than get bogged down in a long drawn out siege which would have forced him to remain in one place long enough for the French to concentrate against him. Given their inability to defeat the English militarily, the French had little option but to sue for what terms they could get: the economy was in ruins, the government had broken down, the fields could not be tilled, the population yearned for peace at any price and Jean would promise virtually anything to gain his freedom. From the English point of view the gains were enormous: it was true that the claim to the French throne had been abandoned, but a third of the kingdom in the hand was better than the whole of the kingdom in the bush. No one, French or English, could have predicted that in a mere fifteen years almost all the English gains would be lost.

The Treaty of Brétigny did not stop war by surrogacy from continuing. In Brittany, the struggle between the Blois and the Montfort factions was finally settled with the death of Charles of Blois at the Battle of Auray in September 1364, when the English army was commanded by Sir John Chandos with Sir Hugh Calveley as his second-in-command. One of the prisoners taken, and who was to make a habit of being captured by the English and subsequently ransomed, in this case paid by the French king, was one Bertrand du Guesclin, a Breton born of impoverished gentlefolk who was the exception to the rule of French social immobility and had come to the attention of the then Dauphin during the earlier fighting in the Breton wars. Eventually, although with no great ability as a general, he would become a great French hero in a land badly needing heroes, would be made Constable of France and be a constant thorn in the side of the English. On the English side Calveley was yet another who had risen to prominence due to his ability as a soldier. A native of Cheshire he first fought under Sir Thomas Dagworth in Brittany and in the guerrilla war that followed was twice captured and ransomed, once at the Battle of the Thirty in 1351 and again as the captain of the garrison of Bécherel. He was a captain of archers at Poitiers and subsequently commanded a mixed force of men-at-arms and archers which became in effect a free company after the Treaty of Brétigny. Calveley and his company served as mercenaries in the army of Pedro the Cruel, king of Castile and an ally of Edward III, in Spain before returning to Brittany. At some stage Calveley was knighted and success at Auray brought him the grateful thanks of the now duke John Montfort and a large annual pension.

In 1361 the Black Prince, now thirty, married his childhood friend Joan, countess of Kent and widow of Sir Thomas Holland, described by the Chandos Herald as a 'lady of great worth' despite the fact that until recently she had been stony broke. This was in many ways an extraordinary match. No heir to the throne had taken an English bride since the Norman Conquest. Dynastic marriages with members of foreign royal families were major diplomatic instruments in the hands of English kings. By contemporary standards, Joan had a racy past. She was the same age as the prince and already had four living children (a fifth, a daughter, had died in infancy). It seems, nonetheless, to have been a genuine love match, and, surprisingly perhaps, to have been approved of by King Edward, for he instigated a petition to the Pope for a dispensation to allow the marriage (the couple were cousins). That same year the Plague returned, and while as in its first visitation it had a less destructive effect in England than in France, it nevertheless slowed down the process of transferring lands to English rule and tying up the myriad bureaucratic loose ends inevitable in such a mammoth transfer of sovereignty. In England the first outbreak of the pestilence had hit the aristocracy less severely than the common people, probably due to the cleaner living conditions and better food of the former, while this time the mortality rate was reversed. Overall the death rate was less – in Bishop's Waltham fifty-three tenants died this time compared to 264 in 1348-49, although there were of course fewer tenants to start with in 1361. In Yorkshire 'only' fourteen per cent of priests died this time, whereas twenty-two percent of tenants-in-chief and twenty-four percent of the lords of parliament were taken . It has been suggested that the class disparity in the mortality rate points to the 1361 outbreak being of a different disease to the previous epidemic, but the contemporary chronicles all say that the symptoms in 1361 were identical to those of the earlier plague, and it may well be that the lower orders had acquired some immunity, which could have been passed on to their children, denied to their betters who had not been in contact with the disease on its first appearance.

In July of 1362, the Black Prince was confirmed as the ruler of Aquitaine, in return for an annual payment to the king of one ounce of gold. Prince Edward, Joan, and Joan's four Holland children all moved to Bordeaux. While English officials and garrison commanders were appointed to the more senior posts, there was little interference with the local administration at the grass roots. It was hoped that the duchy could be entirely self supporting, and given that a long period of peace was now expected and that the wine trade, already lucrative, would presumably become more so, that was a reasonable assumption to make. It had not taken into account the intentions of the Dauphin.

The cause of the death of Jean II in London in 1364 is unknown, it may have been a last flicker of the plague or it has been suggested that rich food and an abundance of alcohol may have had something to do with it. In any event he was only in his forties and his reign could not in any sense have been described as successful. The Dauphin now ascended the French throne as Charles V. Known to the French chroniclers as Carolus Sapiens in tribute to his library of over 1,000 books in the Louvre, he was sickly, of insignificant appearance and no soldier, but he was no fool either. He had no intention of accepting the new status of the English in France, but was too much of a lawyer to attempt to oppose it openly, rather he would whittle away at English possessions and try to undermine their government rather than attempt to confront them militarily, which he was experienced enough to know he could not do – at least not yet. He was a far greater threat to the English than either of his Valois predecessors. The problems facing Charles were reduced when Duke John of Brittany, now put in place by the English, accepted that he held that duchy as a fief of the king of France (as in law he did) and paid homage to Charles for it. In Brittany at least there would be relative stability. That left the problems of Charles the Bad of Navarre, the routiers and the shortage of funds in the national treasury.

Charles of Navarre was a constant threat because he held lands near Paris and could block the routes into and out of that city. He had vacillated between opposing Charles when Dauphin and making alliances with him, and was very much a man who looked to the main chance whatever the rights or wrongs might be. Infuriated by Charles V's bestowal of the Duchy of Burgundy on his son Philip, and insisting that his claim was much stronger than that of the Valois, Charles of Navarre raised a largely mercenary army consisting of free companies, Navarese, renegade Frenchmen and the Captal de Busch and his Gascons, and marched on Paris, only to be roundly defeated by the king's forces and forced to retreat back into Normandy. He had no option but to sue for peace in 1365, but had to surrender all his lands near Paris to get it.

The routiers were a far greater problem. Owing loyalty only to themselves they were well organised, well led and well equipped and preyed on vast tracts of the French hinterland. Made up of Spaniards and Germans and occasional Bretons and Normans, as well as Englishmen, the majority in their ranks were Gascons, but most were commanded by English officers and to the French all were 'English – the scourge of God'. Led by men like Sir Hugh Calveley, Sir Robert Knollys (of Cheshire yeoman stock, he had started his military career as an archer under Sir Hugh Calveley) and Sir John Hawkwood (the son of a London tanner and another ex-archer), all of whom had held commands in the English army but had now been demobilised, the routier companies had strict rules as to the division of spoils, a proper chain of command and in most cases a uniform. They had become accustomed to life as soldiers and to being able to burn and plunder as they liked, and saw no reason to stop doing so just because there was now peace between England and France. As far as Edward of England was concerned, provided the free companies did not profess to act in his name he was perfectly happy that they should exist – the alternative might have been for them to return to England and ply their unpleasant trade there. Although each of the many free companies was nominally independent they did occasionally combine into 'great companies' sometimes numbering several thousand, when they could indulge in undertakings even more ambitious than mere large scale brigandage. At one time a great company under Sir Robert Knollys advanced on Avignon and menaced the pope while another carried out a chevauchée around Lyons. Charles V's France was in no state to put them down by force and in most cases local dignitaries and city authorities simply bought them off. Then a recurrence of the war by proxy gave Charles V his chance to rid France of the free companies.

GORDON CORRIGAN

Chapter Five – The War Goes On

The Iberian peninsula in the 1360s was divided into the kingdom of Portugal, with borders more or less where they are today, Castile and Leon covering central and northern Spain, Aragon south of the Pyrenees and east to the Mediterranean, Navarre bordering on Aquitaine to the north and sandwiched between Castile and Aragon, and the last Moorish kingdom, Granada, in the south. The king of Castile, Pedro the Cruel[*], was in dispute with his half-brother, Enrique of Trastamara, who claimed the throne, a dispute that escalated into civil war. Enrique appealed to Charles V of France for help, and Charles, seeing a chance of striking a blow at the pro-English Pedro and getting rid of his troublesome routiers at the same time, ordered Bertrand du Guesclin to gather together the greatest company he could and take them into Spain to fight for Enrique. Bertrand did just that. He assembled perhaps 10,000 men, a mixture of English, Gascon and Navarese free companies, French men-at-arms and mercenary crossbowmen and crossed into Castile where he collected Castilian supporters of Enrique, deposed Pedro, and placed Enrique on the throne. Up to this point, the Black Prince was not over concerned: Pedro was generally regarded as a nasty piece of work and the Prince did nothing to stop the free companies and his own Gascons from marching off to join du Guesclin. In England, King Edward took a different view. However unpleasant a character Pedro might be, it was not in England's interest to have a French client state controlling the north of Spain. Castilian galleys had menaced the English coast and the routes for the Bordeaux wine trade in the past and might well do so again. When Pedro invoked the treaty of alliance with the English, signed in 1362, King Edward ordered his son to put Pedro back on his throne. The Black Prince began to collect an army which would

[*] As all medieval Spaniards were cruel, Pedro must have been very cruel indeed.

58

consist of his own retinue of professional English soldiers, Gascons lately in the pay of du Guesclin and Enrique, and a contingent from England, mainly archers, commanded by the Black Prince's younger brother, the twenty-seven year old John of Gaunt, Duke of Lancaster since 1362[*].

If the English were to support Pedro with an army from Aquitaine then they would need to cross the Pyrenees, and that meant getting Charles of Navarre, who controlled the mountain passes and could easily close them, on side. This was achieved by Pedro promising him Castilian territory that would allow Navarre an outlet to the sea and a cash grant of £20,000. As Pedro had no money, other than the crown jewels that he brought with him when he fled Castile to Bayonne and threw himself on the Black Prince's mercy, the money was leant to him from the coffers of Aquitaine. In Castile Enrique, now that he was on the throne, saw no need to retain the huge and expensive army that had put him there, and so paid the free companies off except for du Guesclin's Bretons and a force of around 400 English archers commanded by Sir Hugh Calveley. With their severance pay in their knapsacks the companies either returned to Aquitaine, where they promptly took service with the Black Prince's army – they had been well paid to put Enrique on the throne and were quite happy to be well paid to knock him off it – or headed east into Aragon where there was employment in guarding the frontier area against Castilian incursions.

In mid-February 1367 the Prince's army of around 8,000 men started its march up the traditional invasion route from St Jean Pied de Port through the pass of Roncesvalles. Roncesvalles can be treacherous even in summer, and now it was the middle of winter,

---

[*] John of Gaunt had married Blanche, daughter of Henry of Grosmont, cousin of Edward III and the first duke of Lancaster - and only the second duke to be created in England, after the Black Prince (duke of Cornwall, a title born by all Princes of Wales ever since). When Henry died without male issue in 1361 (probably of the plague, having returned to England after the treaty of Brétigny) Edward III created John Duke of Lancaster in 1362.

with thick snow, temperatures well below freezing and not a blade of grass for the horses nor ear of corn for the men to be found. It says a very great deal for the logistic arrangements of the army that they traversed the pass and reached the plains north of Pamplona in good order. We do not know the names of the quartermasters who worked out how much fodder and rations needed to be carried, and who hired the mules and the carts to transport it, but with experienced men like Sir John Chandos, Sir Robert Knollys and Sir William Felton, the latter the son of a soldier and who was part of the Vanguard commanded by John of Gaunt and probably there to look after the Duke of Lancaster on his first serious military campaign, it was an army well accustomed to campaigning in difficult terrain and in foul weather. From Pamplona the Black Prince's objective was Burgos, capital of Castile and sitting on the main communication routes north and south. Enrique did his best to block the river crossings but by March the English had reached the plains before Vitoria.

The Black Prince hoped for a decisive battle at Vitoria. The army was arrayed in battle formation and various challenges were sent out, but if Enrique had not fought the English in France, du Guesclin and his French officers certainly had and their advice was bolstered by a letter from Charles V of France advising Enrique that he should on no account be tempted into a set-piece battle, which the English would win, but rather to delay until the English ran out of food and fodder and had to retreat. What the Castilians could do was fall upon patrols and scouts and it was in one of these minor skirmishes that Sir William Felton was killed. He was in command of a foraging party of around 300 mounted men-at-arms and archers west of Vitoria when he was surprised by a much larger French force. Taking up a position on a knoll near the village of Arinez Felton's little group held off all comers until Felton was killed and the archers ran out of arrows when they had to surrender. For centuries afterwards the knoll was known as *Inglesamendi* – the Hill of the English. Not to force a battle was sound advice, and sure enough in mid-March the Prince had to move, heading south east and then south west to approach Burgos from the east, reaching Logrono on 1 April 1367. Sound though the advice not to engage the English in battle was, politics dictated that Enrique could no longer adhere to it. Against all his better judgement, and against du Guesclin's strongly worded advice, Enrique decided to fight, for if he did not then he would forfeit his throne by default as the population increasingly turned to Pedro.

The Trastamaran army took up a blocking position east of the village of Najéra on the main road to Burgos. In front of them was a tributary of the River Najerilla, which itself flows into the Ebro to the north, while behind then was the Najerilla itself and then the village. There was one narrow bridge over the Najerilla and to the west of the village was (and is) a line of sandstone cliffs, difficult to scale without weapons and armour, impossible with and with no route for a horse. It may be that Enrique, or more probably du Guesclin, chose the position for the very reason that the army would thus find it difficult to run away. It was in any event a good defensive position for an army that was probably outnumbered by that of the Black Prince who would have to attack – and thus reduce the effect of the archers – if he wanted to force the road to Burgos.

The Black Prince had no intention of doing what his enemy wanted. Well before first light the army left Logrono and made a wide flank march to form up on the north, left, flank of the Franco Castilian line. The first indication the troops of Enrique had that the English were anywhere in the vicinity was when they saw banners and pennants fluttering away a few hundred yards on their left. Du Guesclin desperately issued orders to the whole army to swing round to face north, while the English dismounted and formed their usual line of men-at-arms with the archers on the wings. The left hand French division managed to wheel round reasonably quickly, but in the rest of the army panic set in with the second division dissolving into a mass of men running for the village, while some of the Castilian light cavalry decide to desert to the English. Du Guesclin realised that he had no option but to abandon any idea of standing on the defensive: his only hope was to attack the English and hope that his men could run the gauntlet of the arrow storm. They could not. The Castilian heavy cavalry refused to dismount and paid the penalty in dead, wounded and maddened horses, while the light infantry could not stand. The whole thing was over in a matter of minutes, with fleeing Frenchmen and Castilians trying to get across the one bridge over the Najerilla and trampling and crushing each other in the process. The English rearguard slaughtered them as they were trapped by the river or struggled to reach the bridge, now blocked by the bodies of their own men. It was a complete rout, with du Guesclin and nearly all the senior commanders captured. The next morning the heralds claimed to have counted over 5,000 bodies of Enrique of Trastamara's men. English loses were negligible.

Now began the accounting for prisoners and the calculation of ransoms. Many of the prisoners had been captured by the English before, and had not paid the ransoms promised then, which included du Guesclin and Marshal Arnoud d'Audrehem, and some heated discussion ensued. Enrique had not been captured – although unhorsed he had fled on a horse taken from one of his knights, and eventually crossed the border into Aragon and got away into France. For Pedro the matter of who owned which prisoner was academic – he wanted to slaughter the lot as being the sure way to prevent any further trouble from them. The Black Prince demurred: the prisoners belonged to those who had captured them, who were entitled to the ransoms, and in any case the knightly code prevented the killing of prisoners – or at any rate the killing of rich prisoners. The Spanish campaign culminating at Najéra was a spectacular success militarily – once again a professional English army had crossed inhospitable terrain in the depths of winter and had defeated a French sponsored enemy with few casualties of their own. Politically and economically, however, it was a disaster. Pedro began to renege on all that he had promised; he failed to hand over the Basque country around Bilbao, he was unable or unwilling to pay for the cost of the campaign, as he had agreed, and he could not even repay the loan made to him to buy off Charles of Navarre. Most of the Castilian knights had no intention of paying the ransoms promised, and in some cases legal arguments in the courts of Castile and Aragon went on for years. In the event Pedro's Spanish practices did him no good at all, for only two years later he was again dethroned and murdered, stabbed to death by Enrique of Trastamara helped by those whom Pedro had failed to have executed after Nájera. From 1369 therefore, Castile with its navy was firmly in the French camp.

If Pedro was not going to keep his word and pay for the campaign that restored him, then the Black Prince would have to raise the money from Aquitaine, where there were already grumblings about the expense of maintaining the Prince's lavish court in Bordeaux. As even higher hearth taxes (roughly equivalent to rates or a form of poll tax) were announced some in the population began to wonder whether being protected from French occupation was worth the cost. Some of the Gascon magnates decided, rather shrewdly, to appeal to the French king Charles V against the hearth tax. To allow such appeals was entirely contrary to the Treaty of Brétigny, so for the moment Charles simply noted the appeals without doing anything about them. In the meantime he was restocking the French treasury – the extra taxes imposed to raise the ransom for his father were retained – and building up an army. In January 1369 Charles was ready to make his move: he announced that he was going to hear appeals against Edward's taxation policies, and when challenged that this contravened Brétigny, replied that France had never ratified the renunciation of sovereignty over Aquitaine. King Edward, more politically aware than his son, advised the prince to drop the hearth tax, but Prince Edward could see no other way of restoring his finances. When in June 1369 war broke out once more and Charles announced that he had 'confiscated' Aquitaine, the Black Prince was furious, and was caught by surprise. He was in any case incapable of taking the field personally as he had contracted some sort of disease, possibly dysentery, possibly malaria, possibly both and possibly while campaigning in Spain, which had led to further complications and necessitated him being carried everywhere in a litter.

Charles V had taken note of the lessons of Crécy and Poitiers, and well understood that to fight the English in open battle was to lose. Rather he instructed his commanders, including Bertrand du Guesclin, whom he appointed Constable of France in 1370, to whittle away at English power by selective targeting and what in modern parlance would be called guerrilla warfare. Towns with only a small English garrison could be attacked, foraging parties ambushed, supply convoys destroyed, and populations persuaded, bribed or coerced into changing sides. With the huge disparity in populations England could not put garrisons large enough to hold out in every town, and the only answer was to resort to the *chevauchée*. Sir John Chandos was recalled from his estates in Normandy, but was killed in January 1370 in a skirmish at Lussac-les-Chateaux. He was wearing a long surcoat and slipped on the frozen ground. He was either not wearing a helmet, or if he was had the visor up, and a French esquire stabbed him in the face. His was a serious loss as not only was he a highly competent military commander and strategist, but he was well liked in Aquitaine and noted for his diplomacy. John of Gaunt led an expedition through Normandy but while he created a great swathe of destruction he met no French armies; Sir John Knollys burned and plundered his way to the very gates of Paris but still Charles avoided battle and Knollys could only retire. In 1370, the citizens of Limoges transferred their allegiance to the French. This move particularly incensed Prince Edward, as their leader, the Bishop of Limoges, was godfather to the prince's son and had always been considered a personal friend. Such betrayal could not be tolerated and the Black Prince's army of, according to Froissart, over 5,000 men but probably nearer 3,000, laid siege to Limoges. After a month of mining and counter mining the English collapsed the walls and the soldiers poured in. Edward from his wheeled litter ordered a massacre of the population. As the contemporary chronicler put it:

> Men, women and children flung themselves on their knees before the prince crying 'have mercy on us gentle sir'. But he was so inflamed with anger that he would not listen. Neither man nor woman was heeded but all who could be found were put to the sword including many who were in no way to blame. I do not understand how they could have failed to take pity on people who were

too unimportant to have committed treason. Yet they paid for it, and paid more dearly than the leaders who had committed it...more than three thousand people were dragged out to have their throats cut.

They had indeed paid more dearly than their leaders, for many of the nobles who had instigated the change of allegiance were allowed to surrender and were subsequently ransomed, while the Bishop of Limoges, who should in all conscience have suffered a traitor's death, was handed over to the (French) pope. But although Limoges had been recovered, at least for the time being, English France was falling fast. In 1371 the Black Prince, now crippled by his illness, returned to England leaving John of Gaunt as ruler of Aquitaine and the other English territories. But he could not stop the rot either. As the husband of the daughter of Pedro the Cruel, he was particularly disliked in Castile by the ruling Trastamara faction.

In 1372 du Guesclin marched into Poitiers when the citizens threw open the gates in defiance of the English garrison commander and La Rochelle fell when blockaded by the Castilian fleet and attacked on land by du Guesclin. The last real opportunity to recover the situation came when King Edward mustered an army of 4,000 men-at-arms and 10,000 archers to be transported to France in 400 ships from Sandwich in August 1372. Edward was old, ailing and in the grip of a greedy mistress, Alice Perrers, described variously as a sorceress, a wanton and the daughter of a thatcher but more probably of perfectly decent origins and certainly a lady in waiting to Queen Philippa when she came to Edward's attention. Despite his condition the king himself embarked, as did the Black Prince, carried on board on a stretcher, but alas the weather conspired against them. The fleet spent weeks being buffeted to and fro and never able to make landfall until eventually, having been blown back to England yet again, the adventure was called off, at enormous cost.

The following year John of Gaunt mounted another *chevauchée* from Calais and although he created a great band of devastation through central France as far as Bordeaux, he lost most of his horses though hard riding and lack of fodder without meeting a single French army, du Guesclin contenting himself with cutting out foraging parties, stragglers and small patrols. By the end of 1373 most of Aquitaine had gone, with only the county of Guienne, around Bordeaux, and the coastal strip as far as Bayonne holding out. The French had overrun most of Brittany, whose duke had taken refuge in England, although they could not take Brest which remained firmly in English hands, while in the north only Calais and a few garrisons in Normandy remained of the great holdings confirmed as a result of the Battle of Poitiers. The French tactic of guerrilla war and piecemeal reduction was working, but the task of invading Guienne was formidable and despite increasing French and Castilian strength in the Channel, Calais, supplied by English ships, could hold out for far longer than Charles V wanted to spend on a siege. In 1375 negotiations for a truce began, and on Trinity Sunday (7 June) 1376 the Black Prince died in England at the age of forty-six. Had he escaped the illness that killed him he would surely have been as great a king as his father, who followed his son to the grave a year and two weeks later.

By the time of his death King Edward III was sixty-five years old and senile, cantankerous and losing much of his earlier popularity. Nevertheless he was a great king, perhaps one of our greatest: he had dealt with Scotland, recovered English lands in Europe, presided over a genuine revolution in military affairs, renewed faith in government after the unstable years of his father and then of his mother and Mortimer, stabilised the currency, expanded English trade and made England a power to be feared and respected. That it all began to fall apart in his later years does not detract from his greatness.

England has always been at her weakest when there is a disputed succession, an incompetent monarch or a child king. The successor to Edward III was the ten year old second son of the Black Prince (the eldest, another Edward, had died in 1369 aged six), Richard of Bordeaux, who would reign as Richard II. The real power was to be exercised by a council, chosen from Lords, Commons and Clergy, until Richard came of age with the whole edifice supervised by the king's uncles John of Gaunt and the younger earls Edmund of Cambridge and Thomas of Buckingham. Gaunt was frequently suspected – then and later – of harbouring ambitions for the throne himself, and had primogeniture for the English succession not been firmly established by then, he would surely have succeeded, but all the evidence shows that he was a genuine supporter of royal legitimacy and of his nephew, whose magnificent coronation he arranged (at enormous expense).

Despite the wishes of both the ruling council of England and of the French king Charles V for some form of truce, there were too many vested interests in mayhem and murder for fighting to stop completely, and while there were no great battles for the next few years raids, sieges and encounters at sea went on, and although the English no longer got the best of all these skirmishes, the seemingly unstoppable French advance was slowed and then halted. The efforts of those wishing a permanent peace suffered a setback when the French Pope Gregory XI died in 1378 and the conclave of cardinals elected an Italian, Bartolomeo Prignano, as Urban VI. The French refused to accept his election and put forward their own candidate, Cardinal Robert of Geneva, who although Swiss by birth had spent most of his time in France, and acclaimed him as Pope Clement VII. Thus began the Great Western Schism, with Urban in Rome recognised by England and Clement in Avignon supported by France and Scotland. Previously, while the popes were regarded with great suspicion by the English, they did at least provide a forum for peace negotiations, now with the schism that option was gone and there was no professedly disinterested single body to act as a go between.

Richard II was in many ways a tragic figure. As the younger son he would not have been raised to be king. Although his mother had considerable (and generally beneficial) influence on his early education and subsequent development, he had little contact with his father who was frequently away on campaign, and his senior uncle, Gaunt, was unpopular in the country. This unpopularity was of course partly engendered through envy: the dukedom of Lancaster was immensely rich and in many aspects was independent of the central government, while Gaunt's frequent quarrels with various bishops (usually over the question of sanctuary in churches), his obvious disdain for public opinion and his, perhaps surprising given his genes, lack of charismatic military leadership did not help his reputation. It was an unfortunate start to the reign that the truce negotiated in 1375 ran out only a few days after Richard's accession, and it was even more unfortunate that the French had used the brief peace to prepare for war, by embarking on a major ship building programme based in Rouen. Meanwhile, the English, were short of money and much less energetic. In the summer of 1377, French fleets aided by Castilian galleys of King Enrique of Trastamara raided the English channel ports from Rye as far as Plymouth. They would land, loot what they could, set fire to anything that looked as if it might burn and set sail again. They landed on the Isle of Wight and extracted a ransom before departing; they attacked Southampton, where they were bloodily repulsed by local forces under Sir John Arundel, raided Poole and tried (and failed) to effect a landing in Folkestone. On the continent the French admiral Jean de Vienne blockaded Calais by sea while the duke of Burgundy laid siege on land. Fortunately for the Calais garrison, commanded by Sir Hugh Calveley, although some of the outer defences fell, bad weather and heavy rains made mining and the movement of siege engines impossible and the French withdrew, giving Sir Hugh an opportunity to sally out, attack Etaples farther down the coast, and remove the large quantities of wine stored there. In the Dordogne, the duke of Anjou was steadily reducing English held towns. He captured the Seneschal of Aquitaine, Sir Thomas Felton, father of the Sir William who had been killed in Spain, and threatened Bordeaux, only to have to turn back when he found pro English forces in his rear. Brest was under siege, but was reinforced from England in January 1378, while English attempts to capture St Malo and to initiate a campaign in Normandy failed.

Then later in the year 1378 an opportunity to hit back at the French by proxy presented itself, when Charles of Navarre re-entered the frame. Charles, known to history as 'the Bad' had once again fallen out with Charles V of France, for much the same reasons as Edward III had with French monarchs over Aquitaine: Charles of Navarre was a king in his own right, but also held Navarre as a vassal of the French king, and when Charles of France declared Navarre forfeit, Charles of Navarre appealed to England. The council were very happy to support Charles of Navarre on the grounds that any enemy of France was a friend of England, and contracted to send one thousand men for a period of four months, in exchange for the port of Cherbourg. This was agreed and the English duly occupied Cherbourg, although by the time that the army arrived in Navarre, delayed by bad weather and shortage of shipping, the situation had been resolved: Enrique of Castile had invaded Navarre on behalf of his French ally, but when he heard that an English army had landed in Aquitaine and was on its way, he wisely withdrew. As the English troops, under Sir Thomas Trevet, at this time only in his late twenties and who had fought for the Black Prince at Nájera, were no longer required to defend Navarre they embarked on a foray through Castile, reducing numerous Castilian towns, damaging Enrique's reputation considerably and acquiring large quantities of booty before returning to England as Charles of Navarre made his peace with the French, who retained the Navarese lands in Normandy. While the tactical achievements of Trevet's expedition were minor, the acquisition of Cherbourg was a major strategic gain. Along with Brest, Bayonne, Bordeaux and Calais England now had an outpost line of strongly fortified ports with which to counter French naval ambitions and which could serve as springboards for invasions of France.

Charles of France, having at least gained the Normandy possessions of Navarre, decided to try the same ploy in Brittany, and in 1379 declared that he was confiscating that duchy. This time he went too far and the Bretons, touchy about their independence and with no wish to be part of France, took up arms and demanded the return of Duke John from England. Having secured a promise of English military support John returned to Brittany where he was welcomed with acclamation at St Malo. The English army to support him had been agreed at 2,000 men-at-arms supported by the same number of archers for four and a half months from 1 August, but when the English council discovered that they could not afford to pay and transport so many the size of the contingent was reduced to 650 of each arm to be under the overall command of Sir John Arundel, a younger son of the third earl of Arundel who had been part of the relieving force to Brest in 1377 and was in Cherbourg in 1378. The troops duly mustered at Southampton but the weather and problems in finding troop transporters delayed departure and Sir John is said to have billeted his immediate retinue in a convent, dismissing the mother superior's protests that the presence of such a large number of young men might lead to 'an unforgivable sin which would bring shame and disgrace to the nunnery'.

The unforgivable sin duly occurred. Arundel did nothing to stop it (other commanders kept their men under control), and it extended to the soldiery looting the silver from a local church and generally behaving like their modern successors in Aldershot on a Saturday night. When ships were finally found Arundel's men took some of the nuns along with them, no doubt to sew on buttons during the journey, and divine retribution caught up with them when a violent storm raged in the Channel. Most of the ships carrying horses sank, either off the coast of Cornwall or off Ireland, and in an effort to lighten the troopships the men are said to have thrown most of the nuns overboard, and when that had no effect the ladies were followed by the accumulated plunder of Hampshire. Arundel's own vessel ran aground off Ireland in December and he was drowned. Calveley and most of the other captains survived.

So far, while the French assault on what was left of English France had been halted, the amount of money being spent on men, ships and armaments was far from cost effective. This was largely because there was little coordination between the various expeditions, naval and on land. When Edward III was alive, there was a strong king who made decisions, supported by an administration that could carry them out. Now rule was by committee, never a recipe for strong government, and decisions although made in the king's name were not taken on the basis of what was the most effective course, but looked to the course that all the members of the council could live with. Dissatisfaction with the way the war was being conducted and with the tax burden imposed to pay for it eventually boiled over in 1381. The catalyst was the decision in June 1380 to send another expedition to help the duke of Brittany. The king's uncle, the twenty-six year old Duke of Buckingham, would be in command with around 5,000 soldiers, probably in the proportion of 3,000 men-at-arms and 2,000 archers, all to be mounted. To avoid running into storms and to get round the problem of finding enough ships they would be ferried from Dover and Sandwich to Calais, from where they would make a *chevauchée* to link up with Duke John at Rennes. On 24 June the army marched from Calais, creating the usual swathe of destruction as it went across the Somme, to Rheims, south of Paris and then to Rennes, but without meeting a single French army, Charles V having instructed his commanders that on no account were they to offer battle. Buckingham was now running short of money, and a request was sent back to England asking for sufficient to maintain the army throughout the winter and to continue campaigning in the spring. At home, the treasury was empty and after much argument it was decided by Parliament that the government's demand for £150,000, to cover the expenses of Buckingham's army, and the maintenance of the fortress ports (where the garrisons had not been paid for months), and possibly a little to be secreted for John of Gaunt's ambitions in Spain and Portugal (he intended to pursue a claim to the throne of Castile by reason of being married to Pedro the Cruel's daughter), was too much. They would agree to find £100,000: two thirds from the laity and one third from the church.

And then Charles V died, Duke John came to terms with his successor and Buckingham's army was left high and dry with no option but to go home. Although no one knew it at the time, it was to be the last major English expedition of the fourteenth century. For all the great English victories, nothing agreed had lasted, and it seemed as if the war would go on for ever.

Printed in Great Britain
by Amazon

44458245R00047